MW01643985

5647
S. Drexel

Published in the United States of America in 1987
by Universe Books
381 Park Avenue South, New York, N.Y. 10016

© Fernand Hazan, Paris, 1987
© A.D.A.G.P., Paris, 1987

All rights reserved. No part of this publication may be reproduced, stored in a retrieval system, or transmitted, in any form or by any means, electronic, mechanical, photocopying, recording, or otherwise, without prior permission of the publishers.

87 88 89 90 91/ 10 9 8 7 6 5 4 3 2 1

Printed in Italy

Library of Congress Cataloging in Publication Data

Jouffroy, Alain, 1928.
Miró.
(Masters of modern art)
1. Miró, Joan, 1893, Criticism and interpretation.
I. Title. II. Series.
N7113.M54J68 1987 709'.2'4 86—27275
ISBN 0-87663-513-3 (pbk.)

Alain Jouffroy

MIRÓ

Translated by Charles Lynn Clark

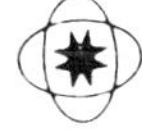

UNIVERSE BOOKS
New York

20th-century painting was invented by artists who were bold and passionate enough to believe totally in modernity. Were they as numerous as is generally thought?

Modernity means running the risk of breaking with the laws of continuity. There can be no doubt that, along with Kandinsky, Mondrian, Duchamp, and Klee, Miró was one of the few truly *modern* painters, in the original sense of the word: those who will not seem "old" for several centuries to come.* Picasso was "old" very early, as was Braque: their works are always loaded with references to classical art. Similarly, Max Ernst built on German Romanticism and Grünewald, Dali on Meissonier. In fact, most of the painters we call "modern" could not paint without referring to earlier artworks. The exception is Miró. He painted without worrying about what had been done before him, identified with nothing, and awkwardly began everything over at zero (or gave that impression) as he hurled himself into the void.

Miró did, however, visit the Louvre when he arrived in Paris in 1918, but felt totally "disoriented, paralyzed." "For four or five months," he later revealed, "I could not even paint." Until then, in Barcelona, he had been painting "realistic" pictures with traces of modernism borrowed from works he had seen exhibited at the Dalmau Gallery. Thrown into the whirl of Paris and confronted with the Louvre, he discovered he had been kidding himself. For Miró, whose points of comparison were Van Gogh, Cubism, and Picabia, the Louvre was like a black hole. Worse, he soon discovered he had no more affinity with the new movements then emerging in Paris than with the Louvre tradition. Dada was the least foreign to his inner turmoil; but what was the point of rebelling, as Dada was, against an order he had never believed in? Miró thus abandoned modernism, which is to modernity what traditionalism is to tradition, and found himself alone in the void, where the Dadaists, then in the process of becoming Surrealists, noticed him... the way someone right-handed notices someone writing with his left hand.

* La Bruyère *dixit.*

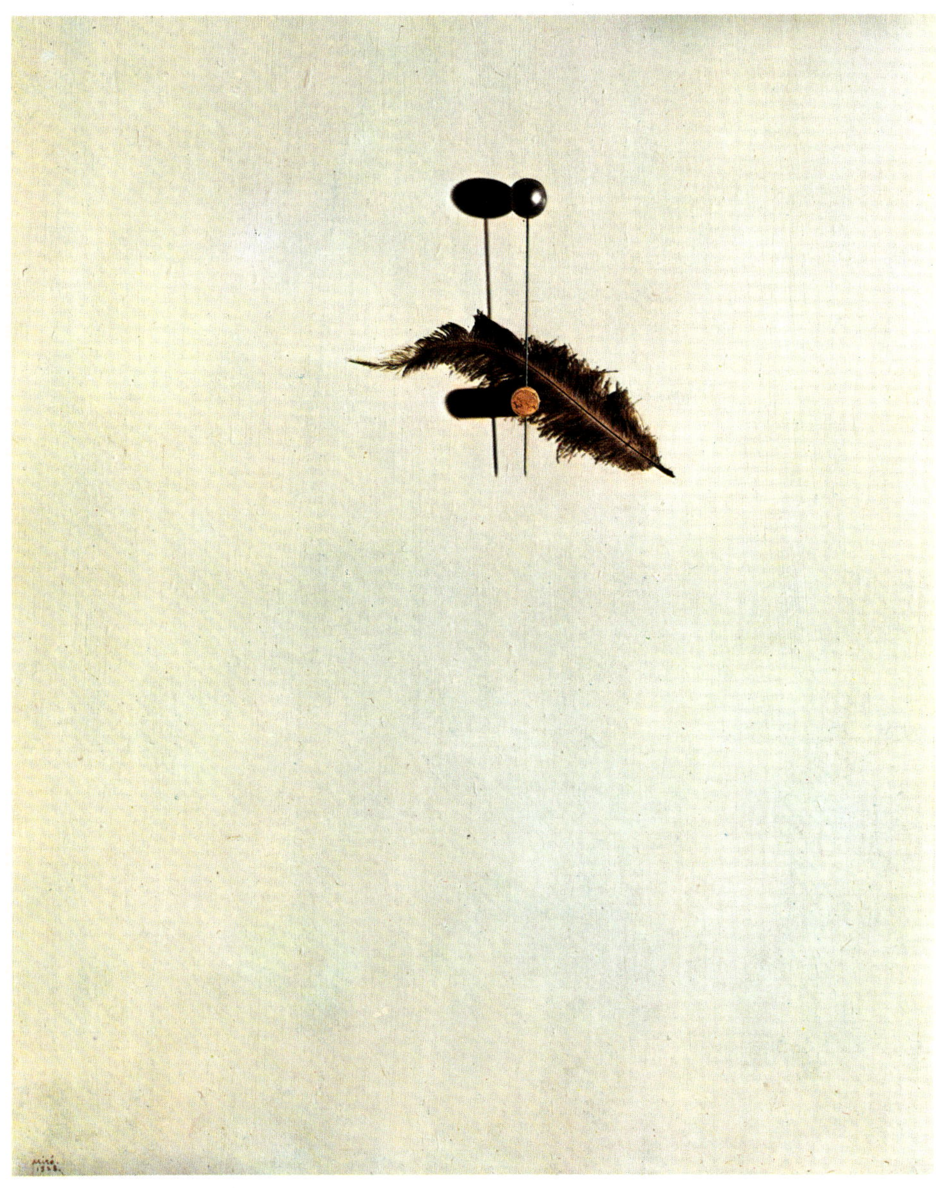

Spanish Dancer
1928

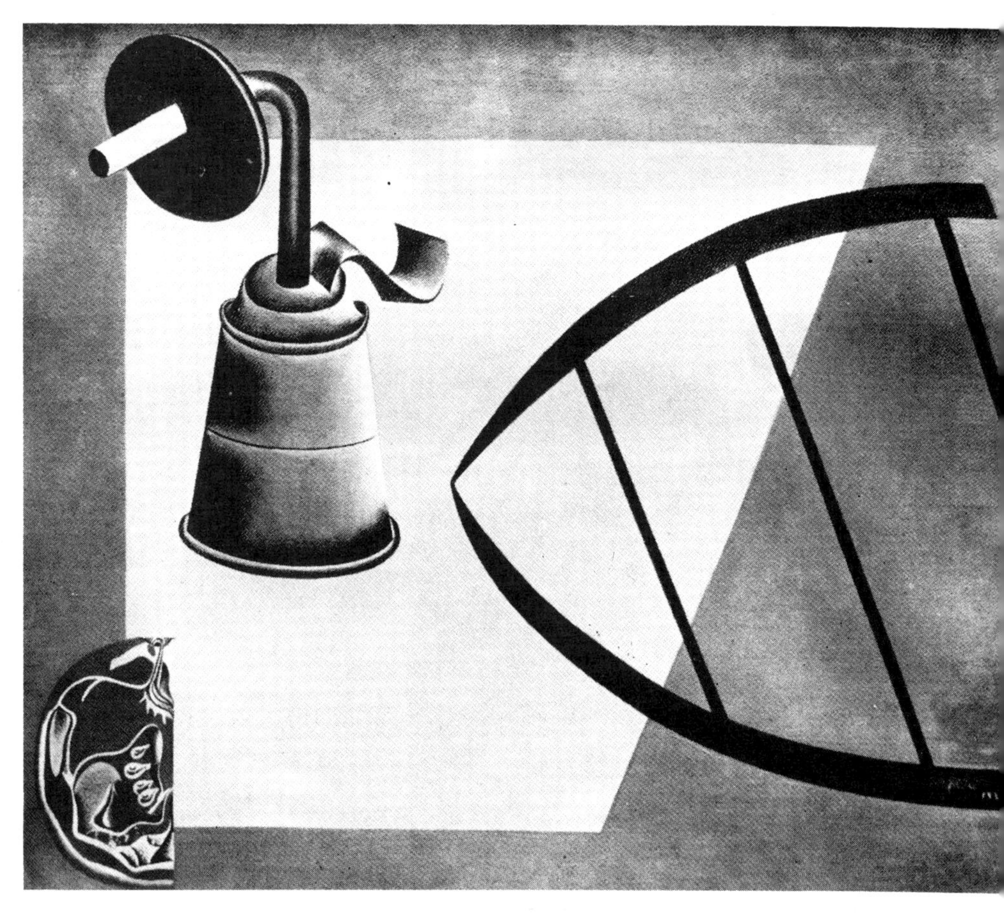

6 | 7

Carbide Lamp
1922-1923

Miró did not go back to the Louvre for ten years. In 1928 and 1929, he went there every afternoon. "It helped me," he said, "by shock or opposition." But he was not impressed by the recognized masterpieces. They spoke too grandiloquent a language for him. His attention was captured by certain Dutch interiors, where he could focus on some "tiny detail—zap! like a fly's eye. For me, that was the key thing." A trip to Holland in 1928 strengthened this interest. Although he had been painting pictures that the Surrealists appreciated for their artless innocence since 1923-1924, he then changed directions and did "Dutch Interiors" in his own manner, followed by "Imaginary Portraits"—*Portrait of Mistress Mills in 1750* (after Constable), *Portrait of a Lady in 1820, The Queen of Prussia*, and *La Fornarina* (after Raphael)—which are anything *but* imitations or parodies. More than anything else, these portraits show the vast no-man's-land separating Miró from all models.

In 1929, when an eminent specialist of modern art interviewed him for the review *l'Intransigeant*, Miró spoke of "assassinating painting" and uttered the often-quoted sentence: "Painting has been in decline since the cavemen." Following the stock market crash, when all anyone could talk about was the "international crisis" and five of his Surrealist friends (André Breton, Louis Aragon, Benjamin Péret, Paul Eluard, and Pierre Unik) joined the Communist Party, Miró, speaking out with sentences like this, dared to say in public what many people were thinking in private.

Also in 1929, Miró temporarily gave up painting and devoted himself to collages in which the unglued edges of the paper were left to flutter in the air. At about the same time, in a similarly derisory vein, he stuck a big pin over a feather in the middle of a bare canvas and called it *Spanish Dancer*; and, using string, nails, and boards, he built his imageless, three-dimensional "Constructions." This man, whom some of his friends thought naïve, sensed the catastrophe hovering over them all.

Thus did Miró enter modernity: through a non-critical reading of the old masters (in the "Dutch Interiors" and "Imaginary Portraits") and a

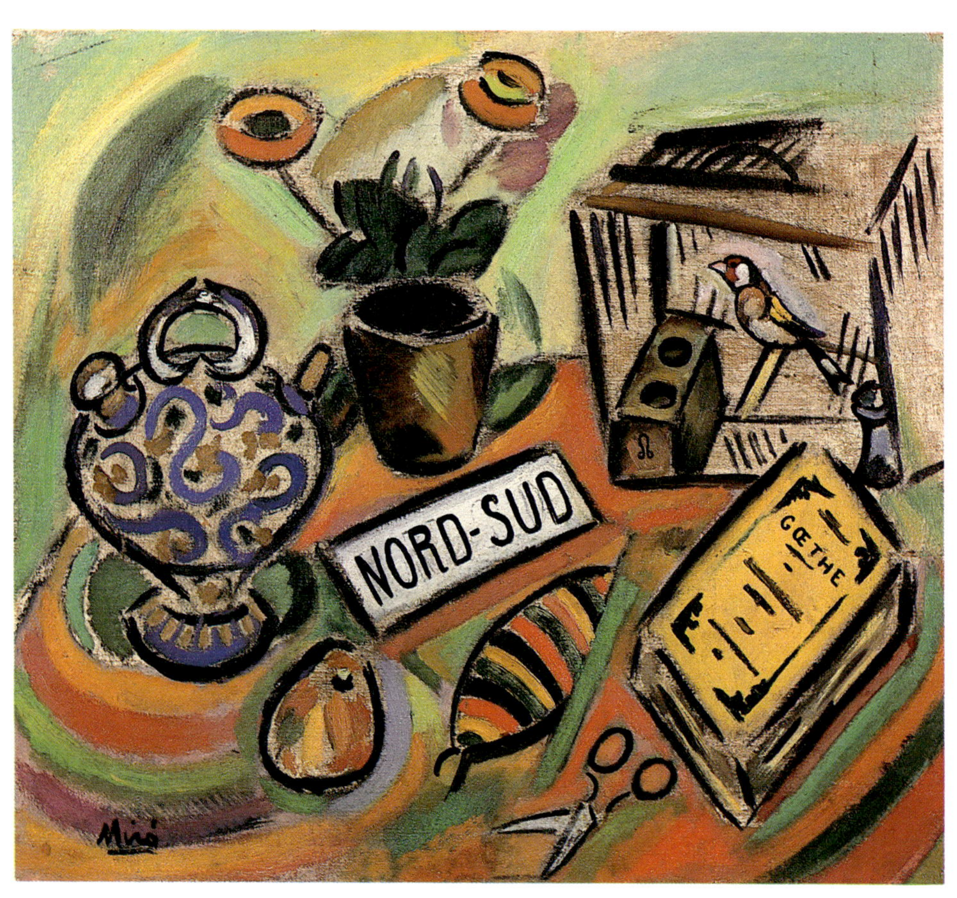

North-South
1917

reduction of the matter of his art to poor materials and ordinary objects (in the "Constructions"). Miró did not become modern by affiliating himself with an avant-garde movement or adopting a preexisting style. His modernity emerged from a silent estrangement, a refusal, an unspoken revolt—not against art, but outside it, in life, or rather on its fringes, where a man cuts himself off from everything that is.

Not yet knowing where he was born, who his father was, why he moved to Paris, or how he became a painter and gained recognition as one of the greatest living artists, not only in Europe, but also in America and the Far East, the reader may be surprised to learn that when Pierre Schneider questioned Miró about the Louvre fifteen years ago, he answered: "Now that I've found balance, I go to the Louvre less often. I can't really explain this logically." There was, it would seem, but one mainstay in Miró's life and work: his own painting.

Instead of going to the Louvre, Miró liked to take strolls—everywhere, but especially along the paths of his island, Majorca. "That's what brings a work to life—walking"; and the problem with most of the paintings hanging in museums was that "they've never been out for a stroll." Pierre Schneider got him to look at the Louvre's display of Tello objects from the fourth millennium. He waited for Miró to speak. Finally, Miró frowned and murmured, as if to himself: "Art? They probably didn't even know the word!" That was his only comment. When they came to Courbet's *Wave*, Miró exclaimed: "It sucks you in, like an undercurrent in the ocean, inexorably. Even if our backs had been turned to it, we would have felt it!"

Miró did not believe in painting because it was Art, but rather the way you believe in a stranger's stare when you suddenly feel it on you, even from behind: an awakening, a shock, a leap, a conquest, a victory over all that is petty and mean. Like a blast of air that forces out everything but the essential, his modernity made him aware of the universe's awesome size and energy. Painting freed him from his own tracks—past, present, and even future. An improvised dance defying the laws of realism, a leap

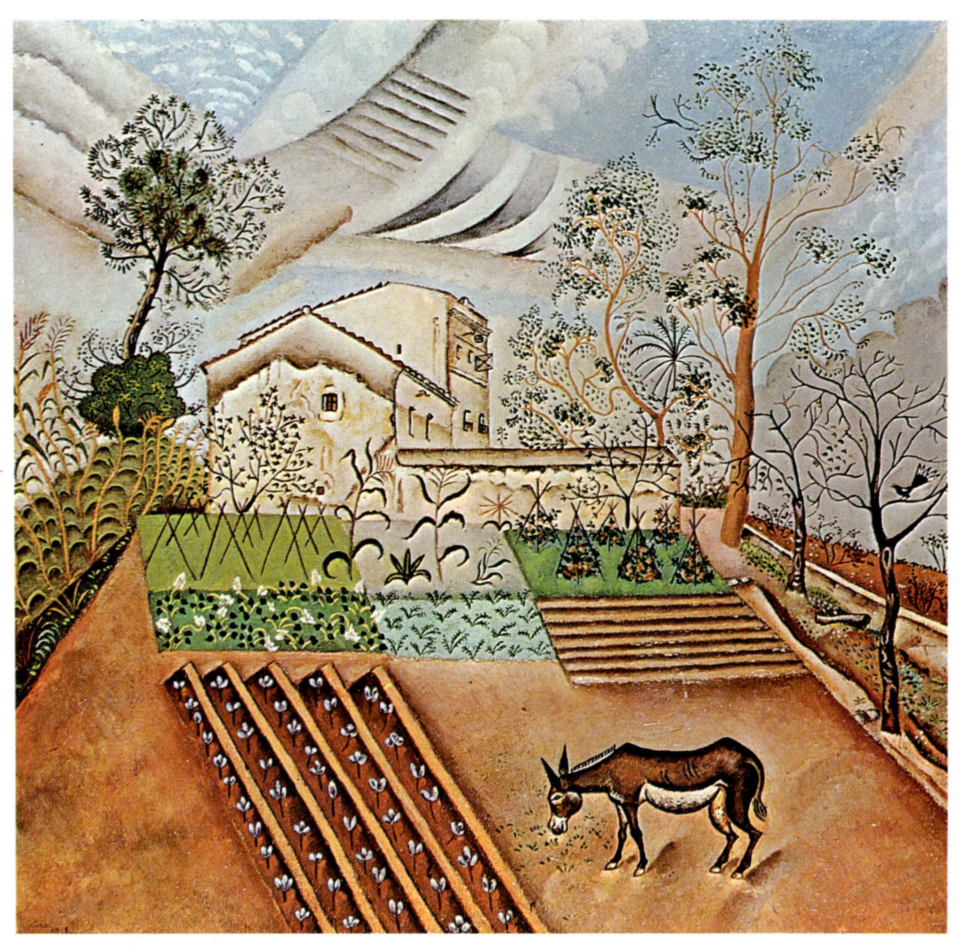

Garden with Donkey
1918

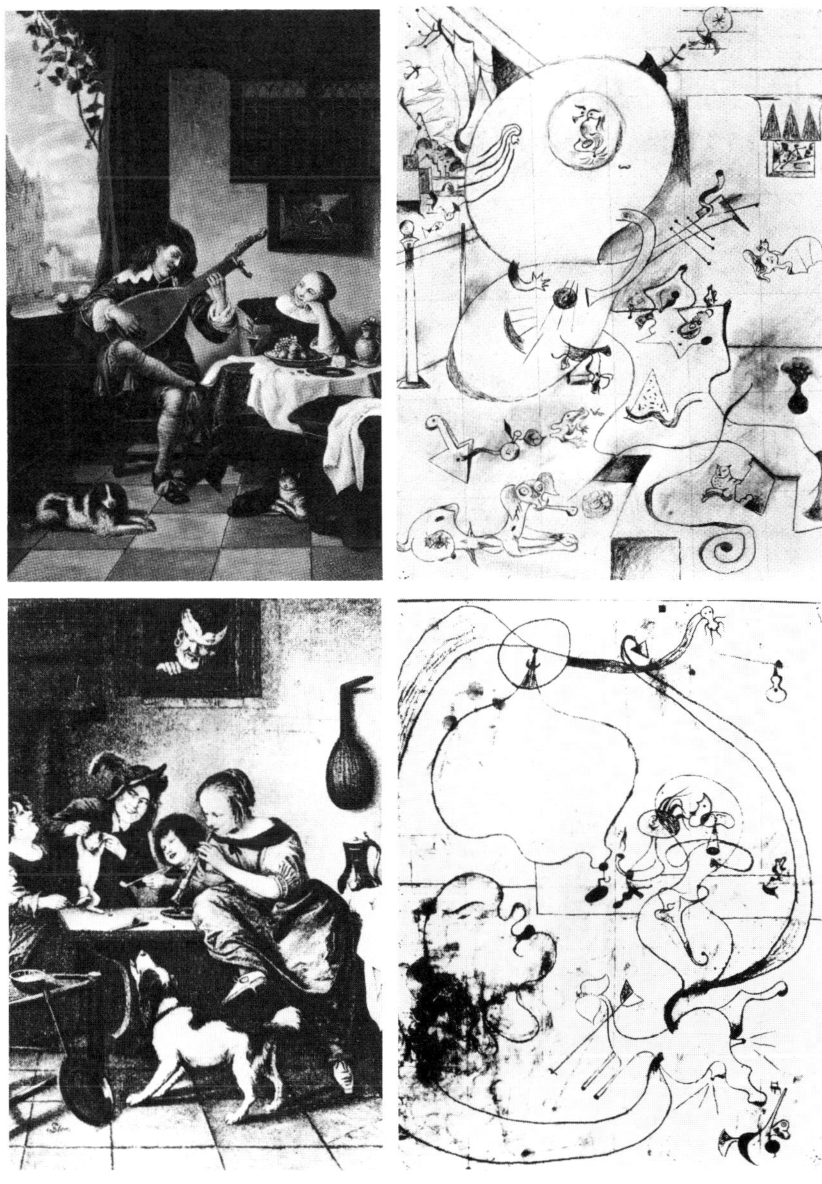

Hendrick Maertensz Sorgh
The Luth Player 1661

Study fot Dutch Interior I
1928

J. Steen
The Cat's Dancing Lesson

Study for Dutch Interior II
1928

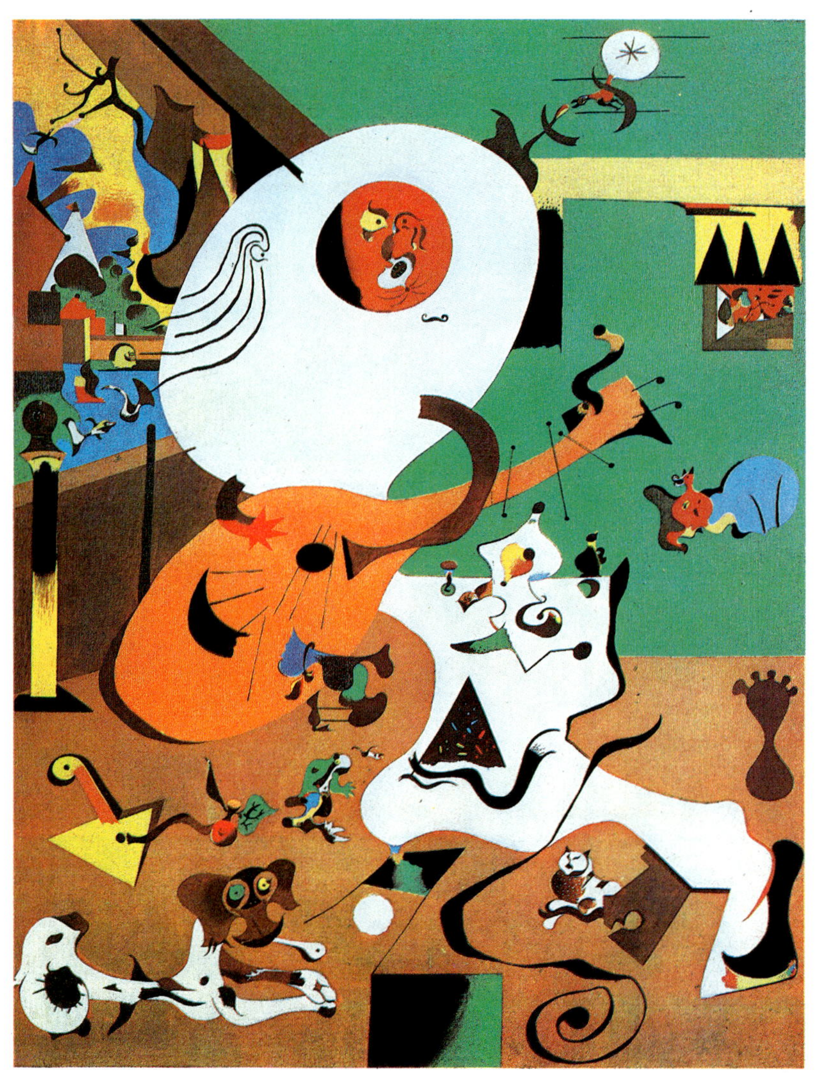

Dutch Interior I
1928

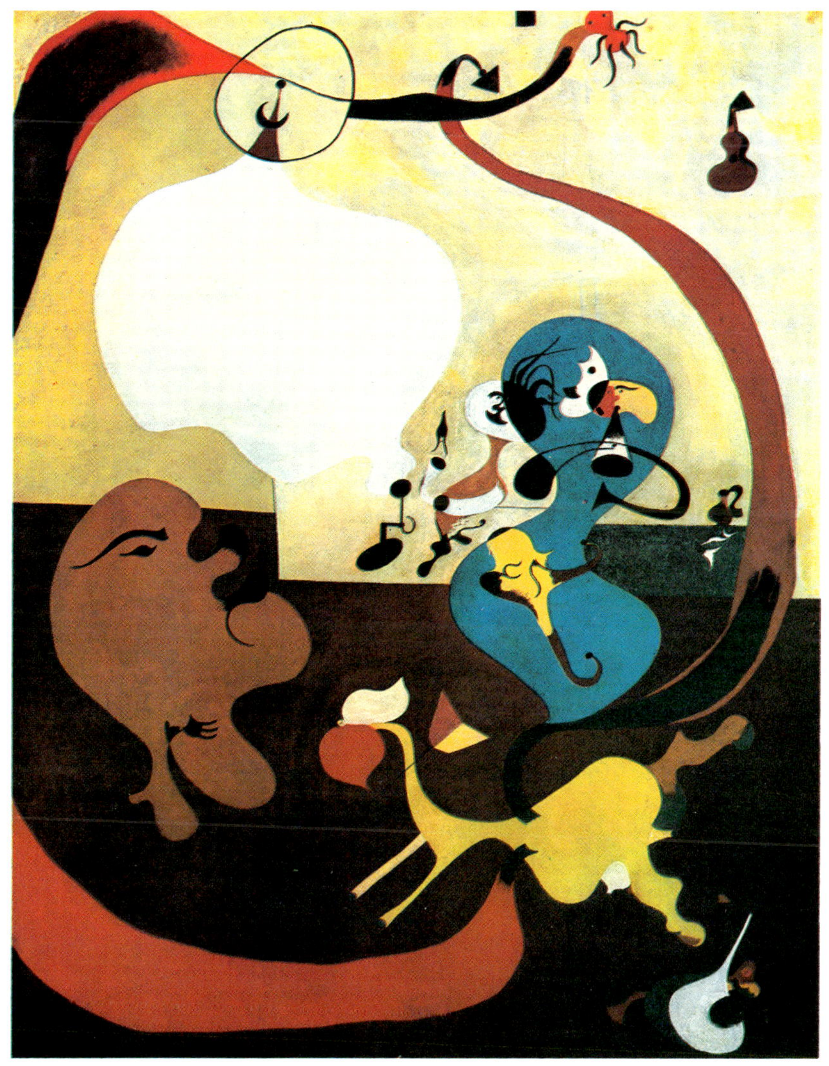

Dutch Interior II
1928

moved, he had already started a series of over a hundred "dream paintings" (to use Jacques Dupin's designation) and continued this project in his new studio. When he broke off working on this series, a blue void inhabited by nothing but a few signs, he did so to paint the "Dutch Interiors" and "Imaginary Portraits," in which, under cover of a return to a figuration of the real, he created a new—his own—surreality.

Surreality is not unreality, but rather an addition, a supplementary expression that dotes reality with a language that can say everything about it, and everything about us. The "Dutch Interiors" are not a dialogue with painting's past, but rather with its present potential, opening onto a future that nothing predetermines. Unlike Duchamp, Miró never drew a mustache on the Mona Lisa. He did not play on the clichés found in earlier artworks. Unlike Dali, he never tried to discover hidden meanings behind the pomp of 19th-century masterpieces such as Millet's *Angelus*. There is no secret admiration, or fetishist imitation, or even iconoclasm, in Miró. For *The Queen of Prussia*, his point of departure was a Diesel motor advertisement he had cut out of the newspaper; on his preparatory sketch, he wrote:

very concentrated
pure spirit
no painting

And, explaining these three lines one day to Gaëtan Picon, he observed: "I painted; but I didn't use the nuances, the recipes of painting!"

It is as if he had chosen old paintings for models in order to prove he could divert them from their ends, deprive them of their status as examples, and make a clean sweep of everything he knew. Miró did not merely take advantage of the "flutter of time that history has created between meaning and silence." He merged with that flutter; and a new meaning emerges from his own silence on history. The original portraits of the Fornarina, the Queen of Prussia, and Mrs. Mills meant no more to him than the picture of the Diesel motor. Miró entered modernity by forgetting all models. Rather than

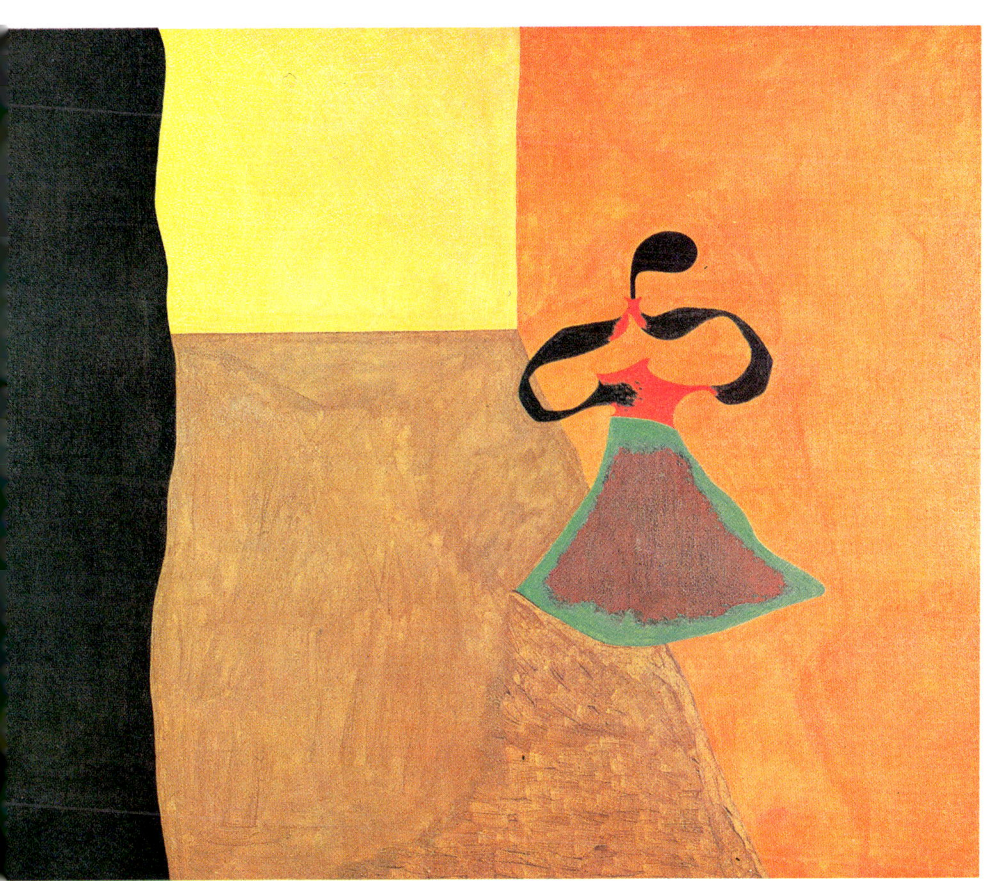

The Queen of Prussia
1929

striving for knowledge, he strove *not* to know. Like someone undressing, he stripped the past of its meaning. He did not simply stop (as Picabia would have) with the picture of the Diesel motor, but going further, discovered lines that no longer corresponded to it. And, so doing, he began to map a world being born: no nostalgia, no looking back, never neo-this or neo-that. Throughout his life, Miró forged ahead.

THE SINGULARITY OF MIRÓ

Even out of friendship for a great theorist, Miró would not submit to theory. When questioned about this by Georges Raillard (*Ceci est la couleur de mes rêves*), he admitted: "I was always a bit suspicious of Breton. He was too dogmatic, too closed-minded. He didn't give me the chance to develop freely. I think he saw painting in terms of ideas. I'm not sure he could deal with surprise. He wanted proof of what he himself had written—that's for sure—to strengthen what he had done as a theorist. Well, theories are completely beyond me."

When Miró lived on the Rue Blomet, his neighbor Masson and the poet Robert Desnos, who often visited their studios, brought him into Breton's orbit. Aragon once told me that he personally had brought Breton to meet Miró. Be that as it may, it seems likely that Michel Leiris and Roland Tual, who also spent a good deal of time on the Rue Blomet, played a part in bringing the two men together. What is certain is that Miró interested all of the Surrealists, who awaited Breton's judgment like an oracle. Until it came, they must have talked about him a lot without knowing quite what to think.

When he looked back on this period in 1941, Breton spoke of Miró in glowing terms: "Miró's tumultuous entry in 1924 marked an important stage in the development of Surrealist art. Leaving behind his earlier works—which, though visually first-rate, were less advanced in spirit—he leaped over the last remaining barriers still blocking total spontaneity of expression. He then began producing works whose innocence and liberty have never been surpassed. It seems likely that his example influenced Picasso into coming over to Surrealism two years later." But Breton's first appraisal of Miró, in his 1928 text "Le Surréalisme et la peinture," was much more reserved, if not downright disparaging: "For the thousand and one problems that do not interest him in the slightest, although they are essential to the entire human spirit, there is perhaps in Joan Miró but one desire: to surrender unconditionally to painting and do nothing but paint (which means limiting himself to the one area we are sure he understands),

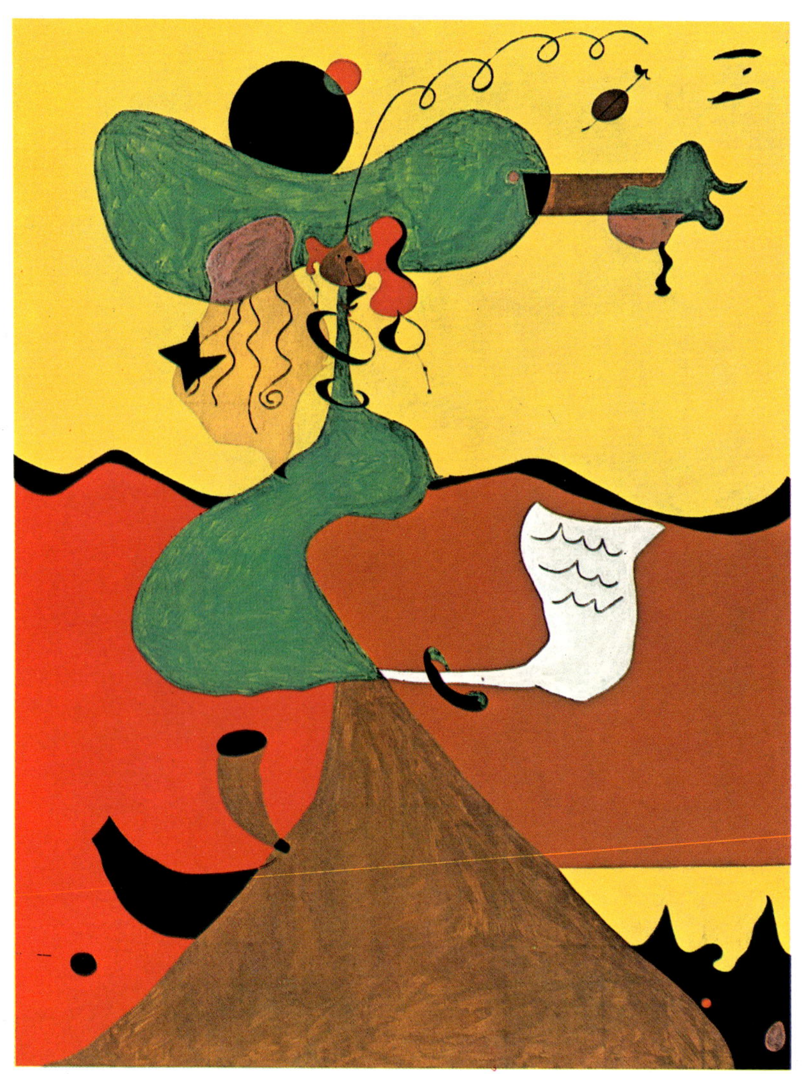

Portrait of Mistress Mills in 1750
1929

to turn himself over to the kind of pure automatism that I myself have never stopped using, but the profound value and underlying logic of which I fear Miró personally has very summarily verified. Perhaps that is why he just might be the most 'Surrealistic' of us all. But how far we are from the 'chemistry of intelligence' we have spoken about!"

In fact, even in 1941, Breton's praise did not keep him from stressing Miró's intellectual limits: "The only drawback to such tendencies," he added to the sentences quoted above, "is that they keep the personality from developing fully beyond the childhood stage, make the artist vulnerable to unevenness, profusion, and play, and limit the intellectual import of his expression." Miró's admirers unfailingly use Breton's contradictory attitude to justify their contrasting of the "pure painter" and the "over-literary" intellectual. And it would be hard to deny that Miró was intimidated by Breton's self-assurance and peremptory judgments. Indeed, without realizing it, Breton was more responsible than anything else for Miró's silence during the Surrealists' daily meetings at the Brasserie Cyrano, which the young painter followed from the far end of the table.

Yet it should not be forgotten, as it all too often is, that Breton could not get around the main fact: Miró gave himself up to "pure automatism," to "total spontaneity of expression," and created with "an innocence and liberty that have never been surpassed." The strangest thing about all this is that Breton found the direct expression of the unconscious to be incompatible with the "chemistry of intelligence," as if the expression of the unconscious were not a superior form of intelligence that dissolves the old antagonism between reason and instinct! But once he had created the myth of a childish, or even infantile, Miró, Breton was determined to stick to it and was still perpetuating it in 1941 when Miró—unbeknownst to Breton, who had taken refuge in New York—finished his splendid gouache series "Constellations."

It took Breton over thirty years to see beyond his initial reservations, which may explain why Miró, "the most Surrealistic" of all the painters Breton discovered in 1924, is often considered by even the most perceptive

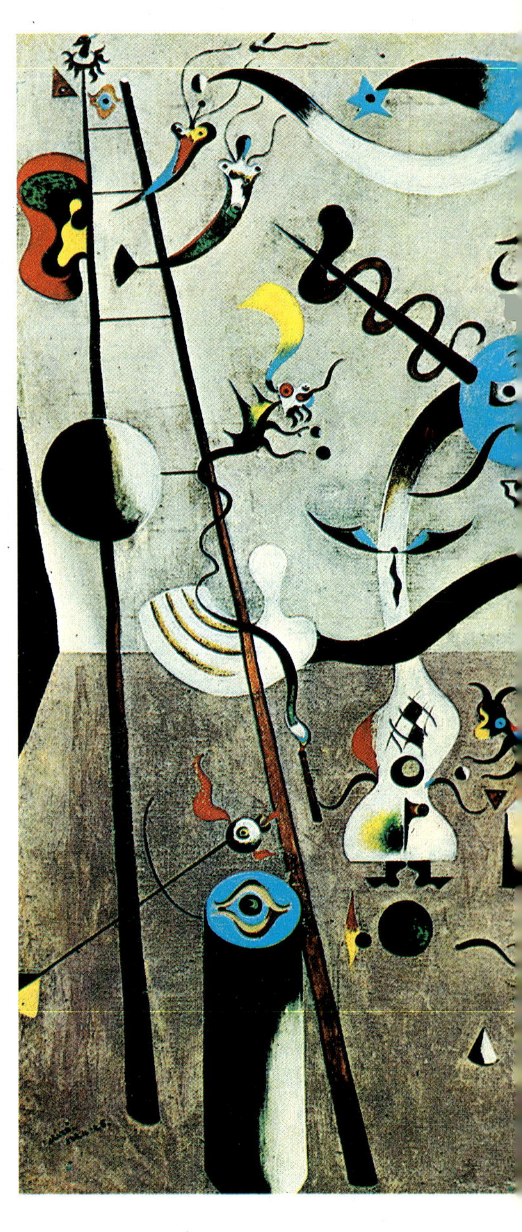

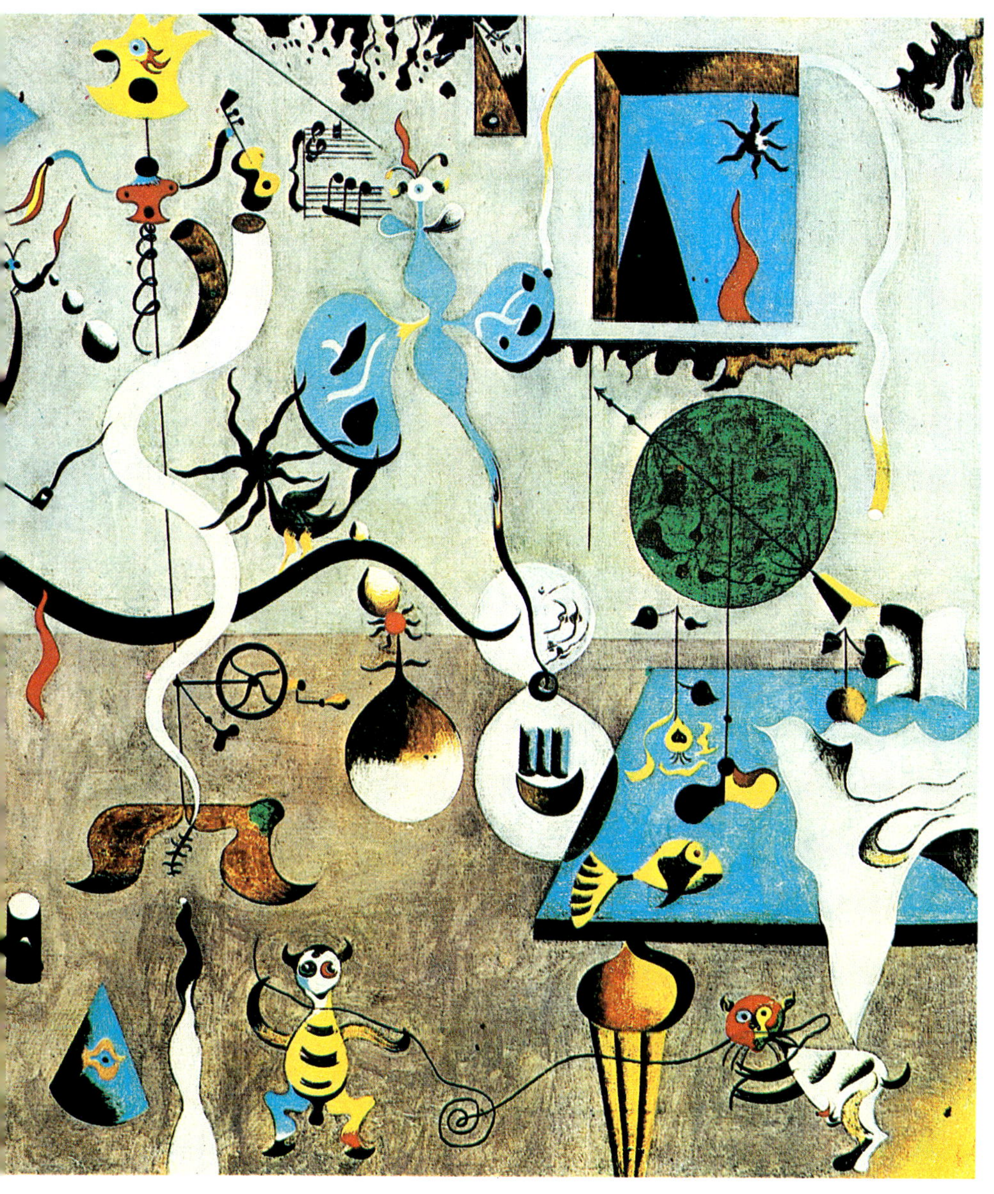

The Harlequin's Carnival
1924-1925

critics to have somehow so totally escaped the movement's influence that he cannot even be described as a Surrealist. Thus, Jacques Dupin, the best exegete of Miró, opposes Miró's "absolute spontaneity" to "automatism," which he sees as a mere "simulation of the authentic dictates of inspiration," a "product of intellectual speculation"; yet, for Breton, as for everyone else who practiced automatism, it was utterly identical to "absolute spontaneity" and "total spontaneity of expression."

Is this distinction just a question of semantics? It does, in fact, hide others: the oppositions between pure painting and literary painting, sensibility and intellect, art and non-art, etc. Miró is exceptional precisely because he somehow invalidated these oppositions, abolishing the frontier separating childhood from maturity and "naïvety" from "intelligence," and short-circuited, from the outset, all of these artificially maintained antinomies. Miró's painting frustrated Surrealism's supporters and opponents alike. Their semantic squabbles became completely irrelevant. His production unfurled with such scope and "profusion" that, as we explore it, we will encounter multiple elements which, while not limited to Surrealism, never exclude it. Surrealism, as a "dogma," is no more limiting than the blind dogma of anti-Surrealism: by agreeing (or pretending to agree) with any and all interpretations of his work, Miró was able to twist both the Surrealists and anti-Surrealists round his little finger.

The misunderstanding between Surrealism and Miró began the day Robert Desnos walked into a gallery at Saint-Germain-des-Près where André Masson's paintings were being exhibited. Desnos did not know Masson's work. What immediately struck him was the "metaphysical" atmosphere in these paintings, which were, in fact, still a bit Cubistic. For Desnos, "metaphysical" meant the climate of Giorgio de Chirico's paintings, which the Surrealists so srongly identified with their own world that they could not accept the fact that Chirico was then changing styles and getting more interested in academic art. A young painter's reflecting the particular atmosphere found in the master's *Disquieting Muses* was quite enough for a man like Desnos to inform Breton immediately. As soon as he

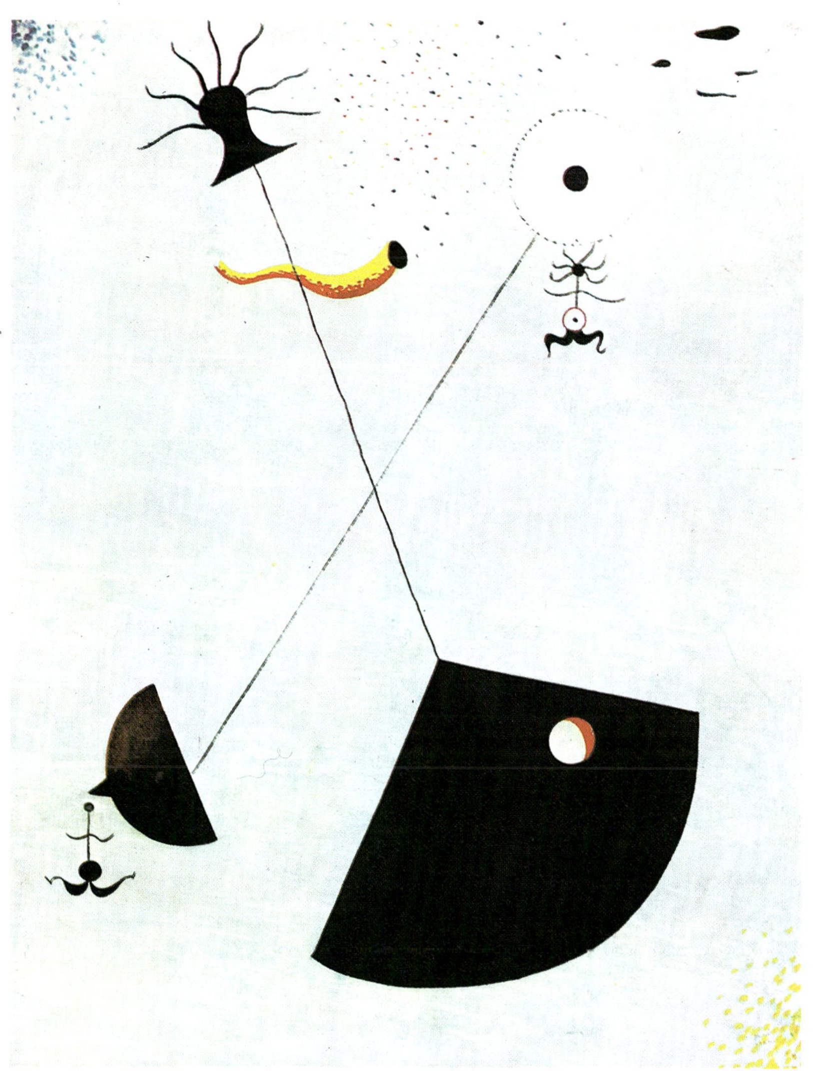

Maternity
1924

had, Breton came running and, just as enthusiastic as Desnos had been, bought one of the exhibited paintings, *The Four Elements*. But Breton did more than buy a painting. In strictest confidence, he told Masson that he and some friends of his were getting ready to found a movement that would be called Surrealism. Back in his studio, Masson mentioned this conversation to Miró, who had met Francis Picabia in Barcelona, without ever really getting to know him. And Miró had timidly enquired whether he "would be better off going to see Picabia or Breton."

Masson, who realized that Breton was no longer as close as he had been to Tzara and Picabia, replied (and his answer says a lot about the sense of opportunity of young painters and their need to link themselves to what is coming rather than to what already exists): "Picabia's already the past. Breton is already the future." One thing leading to another, Desnos and his friends soon turned up at Miró's studio; then, one day, André Breton came to see for himself. Miró's studio was as clean and tidy as Masson's was messy. In the courtyard, there was even a lilac bush, which added to the impression of a country haven the city had not quite devoured. When he saw Miró and his paintings, Breton was speechless. He was prepared for anything *but* that.

The Tilled Field and *Pastoral*, which happened to be in the studio that day, had nothing to do with Cubism or metaphysical painting. Miró differed from Masson in every way. The shock was complete. As Miró said nothing, Breton finally gave up and went next door to talk to Masson about what he had just seen; Masson spoke highly of his neighbor, the way one does to help somebody out who has trouble speaking for himself. The scenario of what Breton and Miró's future relations would be was written that day: Masson would play the "chemist of intelligence," Miró "pure automatism"; but, between Breton and Miró, there would never be anything but the ambiguous silence that separates a master from his new student.

This peculiar relationship may explain why, in 1928, Breton thought he had the right to warn Miró that he was his own worst enemy: "Pure

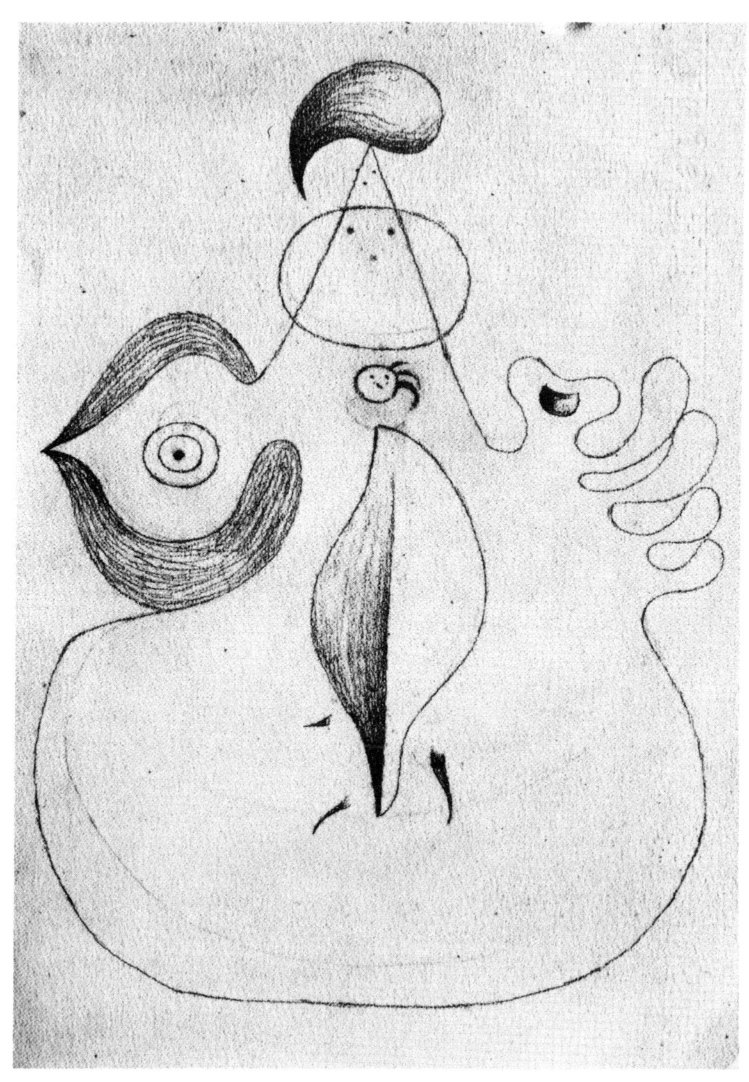

Drawing
1930

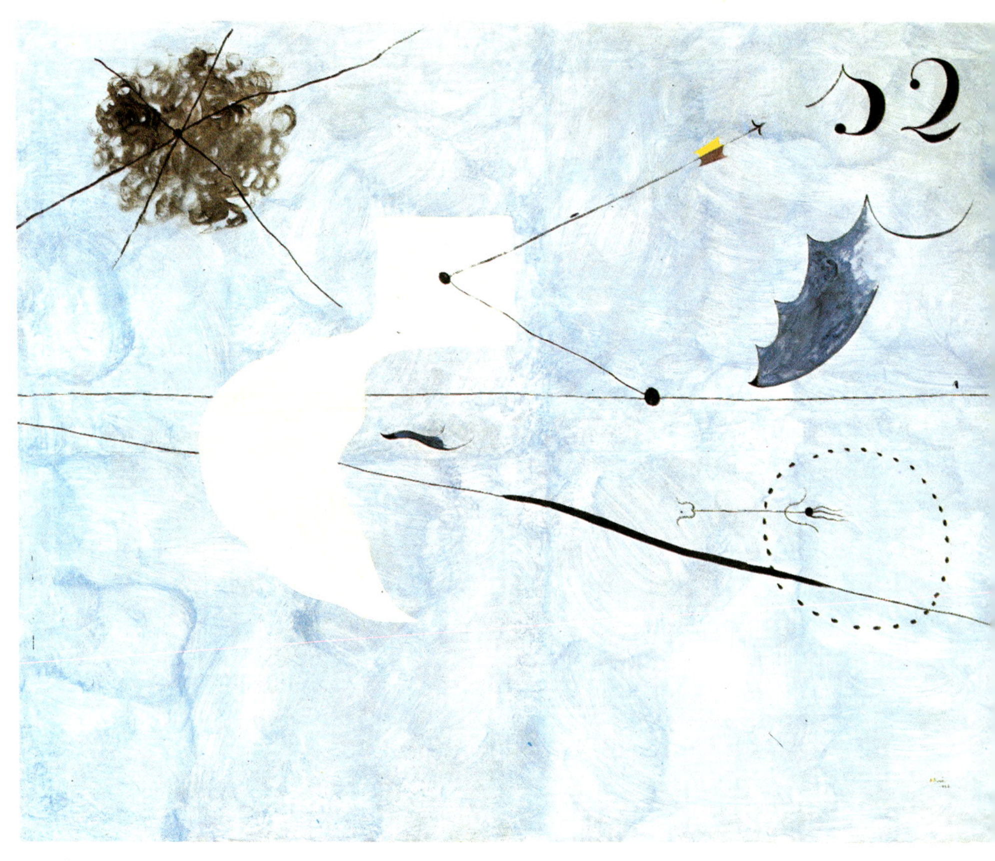

The Siesta
1925

imagination is the only mistress of what it appropriates for itself from day to day; and Miró must not forget that he is but its instrument. Whether he like it or not, his work involves a certain number of general notions that others have also been exploring. It would be vain to hold these notions, as they now stand, for mere subjective concepts incapable of taking on a new objective reality outside of the mind that conceives them. Whatever a few idiots may think, I must affirm here that there are certain imprescriptible rights other than those of painting; and, in spite of everything, I hope that Miró will not contradict me if I assert that he has other concerns than to procure gratuitous mental or visual pleasure for anyone at all." Not only did the hypersensitive Miró never forget this lesson in Surrealist ethics, he imaginatively strove to get around it in his work, up to the day at the end of World War II when Breton, finally seeing the gouache "Constellations," realized how seriously mistaken he had been in underestimating the intellectual powers of one of the greatest inventors in 20th-century painting.

Miró never forgot Breton's attitude—it rankled with him to the end—which proves just how deeply Breton had hurt him: "I reacted with a certain sadness and, especially, indifference to the things you have reminded me Breton said about me," he told Georges Raillard. "His judgments were not straightforward, always ambiguous. But I never confronted him about what he said. Never. When he spoke, he was so brilliant, so dogmatic, that it didn't seem worth trying." Indeed, Miró went on painting as if Breton had said nothing, which is why every last one of his paintings is a refutation of theory. Trusting his own eyes alone, he invented a Surrealist territory of which he was the only master. For once, it was theory that had to adapt itself to the painter's venture, and not the other way around.

"Even outside painting, I always find precocious children, the ones called 'good students,' disturbing," Miró said. In any case, the extremely unprecocious Miró had most surely not received his gifts straight from heaven. With tenacity, patience, and extraordinary will power, he extracted them from his inmost depths. That was, no doubt, hard to see in 1923-1924, when Miró, not yet having come into the Surrealist sphere of

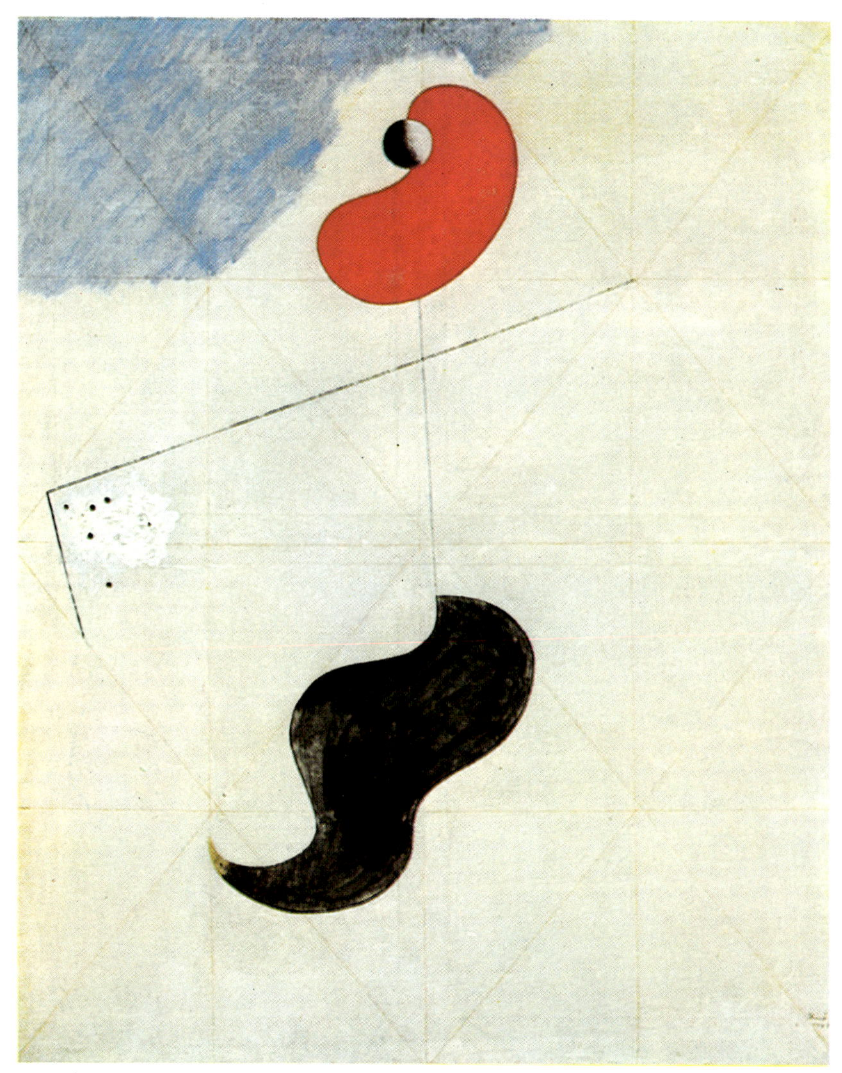

The Catalan
1925

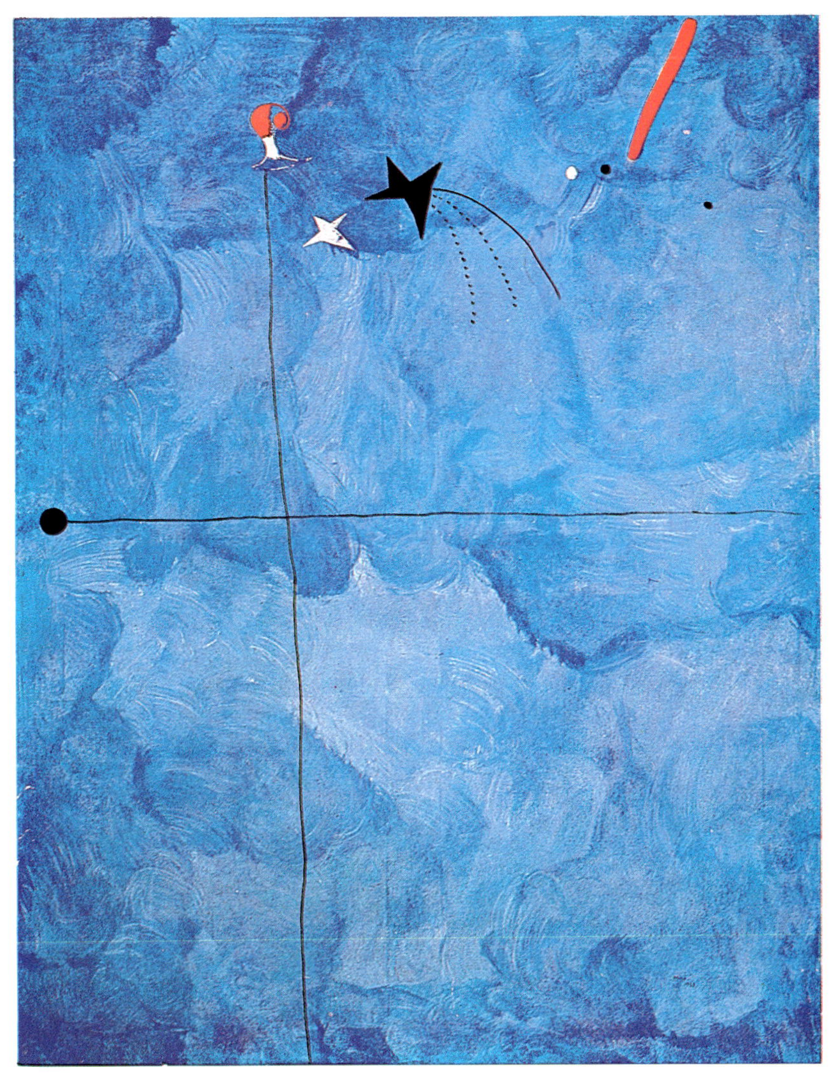

Head of a Catalan Peasant
1925

influence, showed the pictures he had painted in Spain. *The Farm*, for example, reveals Miró's perfect mastery of his art. Everything is placed with accuracy; the coloring is perfect; every last detail is poetic. Everything is there, nothing missing... And yet, something *is* missing: and that something is what was to lift Miró out of his origins as a Catalan painter.

The story of the difficulties of his youth sheds a little light on the tenebrous challenge he had set himself. It is as if something that prevented him from doing things "the easy way" had been growing inside him from the start. This original block makes one doubt the validity of the myth of the sovereign "genius," which Picasso so largely contributed to keeping alive. For Miró, if genius existed, it was in a subterranean way, like the flower and fruit inside the seed.

One need only look at the awkward, but industrious, drawings he did as a child and compare them to his first pictures—neither Fauve nor Cubist, zigzagging and sometimes a bit contorted, as if Miró were struggling to get out of the forms he was painting—and see how, one after another, these pictures slowly led to the mastery found in the almost too well-done, if not overpolished, 1918-1919 pictures—*House with Palm Tree*, *Garden with Donkey*, *The Rut*, *Montroig: The Church and the Village*—to realize that Miró's first necessity was to assure himself, to prove to himself that he could capture form and was not only gifted for color. Painted in 1921-1922, *The Farm* is but the crowning moment in this determined quest for formal perfection, which, though it kept slipping away from the artist, like reality itself, he refused to abandon before 1922-1923, when he was absolutely sure he had grasped it, conquered it, smashed it.

Was this quest, as Breton suspected, just a game ? If so, consisting as it did in work, self-discipline, and constantly striving to advance, it was a very odd game indeed! Some light might be shed on the nature of this "game" by recalling—as art historians delight in doing—the artists who influenced Miró at this time; but, as is sometimes all too visible, it was Miró's inmost self that suggested the successive changes of forms which led to the three pictures

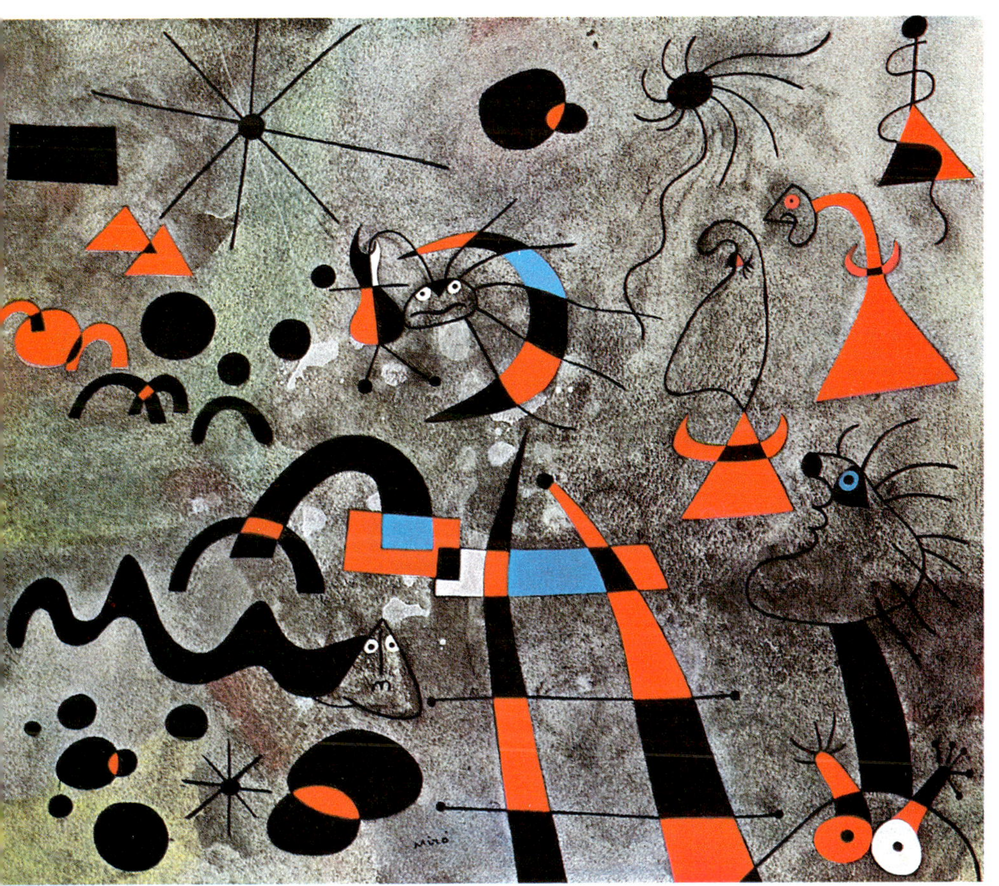

The Escape Ladder
1940

painted between Paris and Montroig in 1922 and 1923: *Grill and Carbide Lamp*, *Carbide Lamp*, and *Ear of Grain*.

When Georges Raillard asked him if his only interest had been plastic transformations, Miró answered categorically, as if he were answering Breton through an intermediary: "The expression 'plastic transformations' automatically implies a transformation of ideas." And when Raillard insisted, to see if Miró really believed in the artist's role in transforming society: "Of course I do," he said tersely, a bit annoyed, as if it were absurd to imagine that anyone could think otherwise. But, unlike Breton, Miró restrained his ideas, the way some people restrain their feelings. Rather than putting them into words, he showed them in his pictures, which it is thus fitting to read in terms of the desire he did once verbalize as being "to open doors onto a different future, against all cant and fanaticism."

Such a grandiose idea might seem out of keeping with the expressive goals of a painter as timid, modest, and craftsmanly as Miró. But it should not be forgotten that the Spanish painter belonged to the Catalan minority. "We Catalans," he once told J. J. Sweeney, "think you have to have your feet solidly planted on the ground before you can leap into the air. The fact that I come down to earth from time to time allows me to jump even higher the next time." This contradiction between the lowest depths and the highest heights, which Miró resolves in a single sentence, says everything. In his pictures, Miró expressed it in the repetition of the ladder theme: already found in *The Farm*, it is often found later, up to *The Escape Ladder* in the "Constellations." In a way, Miró could be said to have painted on a ladder that allowed him to climb down to the ground or up into the sky as he pleased. His brush, easel, and canvas were his ladder, painting the medium of his escape.

Ever since Charlemagne reconquered Catalonia in the 9th century, and the Catalans sealed a sort of brotherly pact with the French that, in addition to other particularities, differentiates them from other Spaniards, five or six million people living on western Spain's Mediterranean coast have been driven by the same passionate desire for independence and, in spite of numerous invasions, have managed to preserve their language and culture (much more successfully than other minorities, e.g., the people of Languedoc). The conquerors of the Balearic Islands, the Kingdom of Valencia, Sicily, and Sardinia in the 13th and 14th centuries, if the Catalans had to turn their authority over to the Castilians, they did not do so with resignation. In the 19th century, Catalonia was already the most industrialized province in Spain and, as such, the first to feel the effects of "modern life." In 20th-century Spain, the Catalan culture has acted as a strong catalyst—so strong, in fact, that Franco was unable to reconquer Barcelona before the end of the civil war, in January 1939. More Catalan than the Catalans, Miró shared this spirit of constant resistance which may pretend to give way, and backs down when necessary, but only to speak out more forcefully later.

As a child, Miró admired a single genius: the architect Antoni Gaudi, who invented a style all his own in the *Sagrada Familia* church and Parque Güell. Gaudi was born near the village of Montroig (red mountain in Catalan), where Miró moved at age ten. The son of a goldsmith and grandson of a blacksmith (on his father's side) and a cabinet maker (on his mother's side), Miró did not see the immensity of the *Sagrada Familia* as an example, but rather as a ladder: proof that a modest man can someday reach the sky. The village of Montroig looks down on the sea from on high. For many years (except during the civil war), Miró returned every summer to this region, whose farms, landscapes, and objects had inspired him in those first paintings he had so much trouble doing. He never forgot the village artisans of his youth. He looked back with respect, but never got sentimental (as people with lower middle-class origins sometimes do) about his family itself.

Everything opposed him to his father, Michel Miró Adzerias, who, projecting his own failures onto his son, attempted to thwart his desire to become a painter. "There was an an insurmontable barrier between my parents and myself," Miró said. "And I'm very happy there was, because

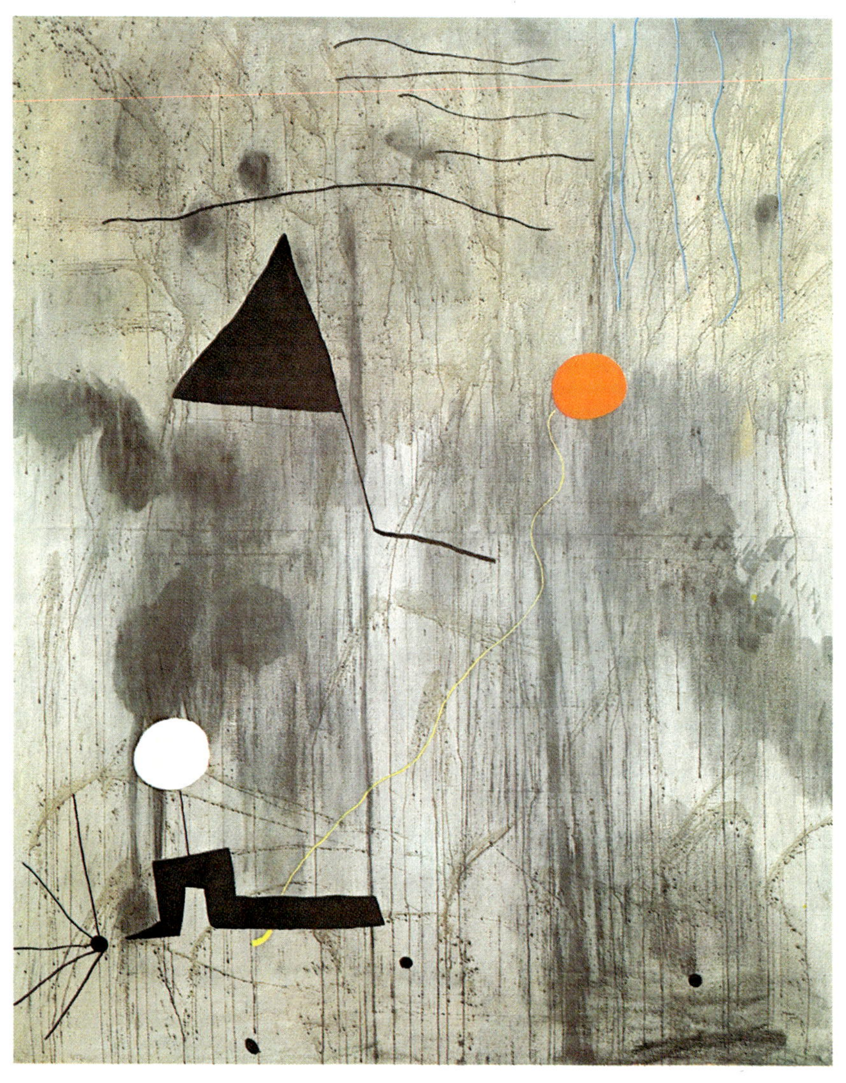

The Birth of the World
1925

when I met the fellows who came to Paris when I did in 1918, fellows from good families, they were already through. The life I had as a child toughened me up. I'm very, very glad it did. I had a very hard childhood, and that helped me a lot." The humiliations he endured steeled his character. His father making fun of his sensitivity when the little Miró went into a rapture over a violet sky made him "burn with rage."

He found school unbearable. A poor student, he was good only in geography, but attended the optional drawing classes with silent fervor, as if he were carrying out a "religious act." During summer vacation, he continued to draw, with an alarming concern for exactitude, trees, tufts of grass, stone walls, houses, churches, village streets, and the rest of the decor of his daily life, where the only thing that stimulated him was to be found in the drawings that emerged before his eyes. All this time spent drawing—in a rather stiff and formal way, as if he were trying to become an "adult" as fast as possible—made him less and less capable of keeping up with his studies; furious, his father put him in a business college in 1907. The stubborn Miró enrolled simultaneously for drawing classes at the Lonja School of Fine Arts, but had trouble adapting to a program designed to train decorators and architects more than painters. Even so, for the first time in his life he received encouragement: Modesto Urgell and José Pasco were the first teachers to sense that this young man would become a painter. It took a lot of intuition; for, incapable of copying from the antique or drawing an anatomy, he would just get bogged down in his efforts.

"I was as clumsy as they come," Miró remembered. His refusal of order and the rules of academic painting was unconscious. Mad with the need to express himself, in revolt against an authoritarian father, he could not adapt to any means of expression that had been defined by others. Increasingly displeased with his son, Miró's father found him a job as a ledger clerk in a colonial trading company in 1910; after moping and fretting for two years there, Miró fell seriously ill. Only then did his family finally give in. After a stay in Montroig to recuperate, he went to Barcelona and enrolled in Francisco Gali's Escola d'Art, a sort of "anti-academic academy," to use

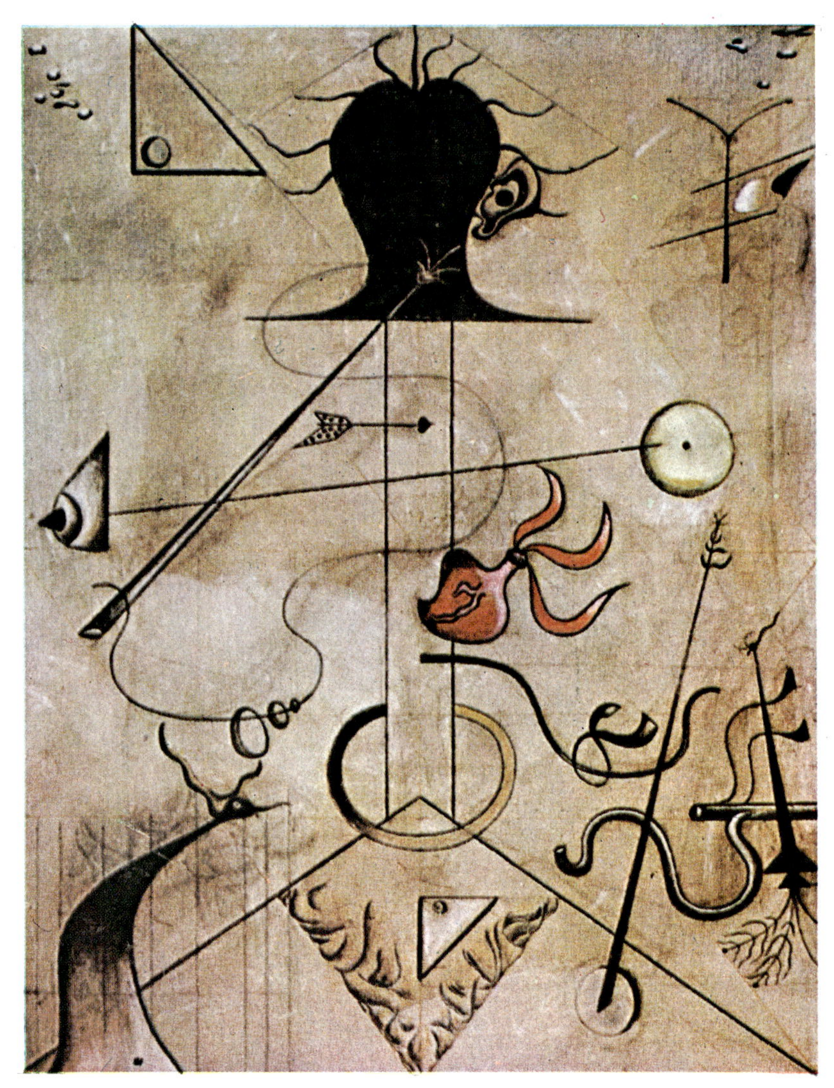

Portrait of Madame K.
1924

Jacques Dupin's phrase.* Fortunately for Miró, Gali was something of an eccentric. When he took his students out to the country, Miró once told me, he would forbid them to sketch during their walks and then have them draw from memory the landscapes they had seen. Gali observed Miró; and, seeing the hostility of his classmates, who thought themselves quite superior to the impossibly clumsy Miró, he told them bluntly: "He's the one who's going to succeed." He even repeated his prophesy to Miró's sceptical father, who was far from reassured. How can we even begin to understand the difficulties faced by a child desperately trying, in spite of his apparent lack of talent, to become a painter ? "As far as form goes," Miró said, "I was a wash-out. I couldn't even tell a staight line from a curve!" To help him, Gali perfected his teaching method based on drawing from memory. He had him feel objects behind his back and then draw them, sight unseen, by remembering what he had felt! The results were convincing. For the first time, a sense of volume and proportion appeared in Miró's drawings ... as if *sight* itself had been keeping him from drawing!

Did not everything destine Miró to paint from the "inner model" that Breton, several years later, told painters they should substitute for exterior models once and for all ? Miró's background would also seem to explain why he did not need any "theory" to become "Surrealistic" before everybody else. The surprise that Miró created on canvas is surely linked to the non-retinal origin of his drawing. His was not an optical, but rather a global corporeal and sensory memory. His unconscious was both psychical and physical.

This particularity created the profound misunderstanding that separated Miró from Breton for so long. In point of fact, neither of them realized that purely automatic drawing is not a question of plugging the hand's movements into the psychical unconscious, but of implementing a displacement from the psychical to the physical level and thus enriching the powers of

* *Miró,* by Jacques Dupin, Paris, 1961.

visual thought through the body's momentum and uncontrolled drives. Just because Miró hated to argue for the sake of argument and criticize for the sake of criticizing does not mean his development had been halted at the "childhood stage." On the contrary, the child in him—the child who resisted school, academic teaching, and his father's orders—formed and, one might say, sculpted from within the adult who conquered the grace of expressing himself as no-one had before and invented, before the expression had been found, Surrealist painting, the possibility of which Breton had not even imagined in his first *Surrealist Manifesto*. But, how could a man of the verb—who thought that automatism was "verbo-auditory," thus hardly compatible with the elaboration of a picture—even begin to imagine a kind of painting that obeys, psychically as well as physically, pure automatism ? In Breton's eyes, all of the painters he had known up to that time—Derain, Picabia, Picasso, Duchamp, Max Ernst, and Masson—seemed more aware of the "intellectual drama" and "crisis of values" than Miró. If we complete this list with Chirico, who was also the author of a masterpiece of humor (*Hebdomeros*), we can understand why Breton had his doubts about the birth of "automatic" painting; but, as he often told me, it was one of the paradoxes of history that Miró was the first to convince him of its possibility.

All of the choices made by painters at the beginning of the century were tied to their close observation of intellectual and artistic trends: Picasso said that Cubism was invented in reaction against Renoir, whose works were enormously successful in 1910; similarly, Masson realized the danger of becoming an epigone of Cubism in 1921, just when Picasso and Braque were themselves enjoying great success. But Miró, who can be suspected less of calculation and scheming, became a Surrealist by following his own momentum and inner contradictions alone, thus clearing the way for the others, who had trouble following because the new path was predetermined by nothing: by neither Cézanne, nor Gustave Moreau, nor the Fauves, nor the Cubists, nor Giorgio de Chirico. It took a wonder of clumsiness to redefine the givens of painting. When Miró came into the game, the treatment of the pictorial surface changed.

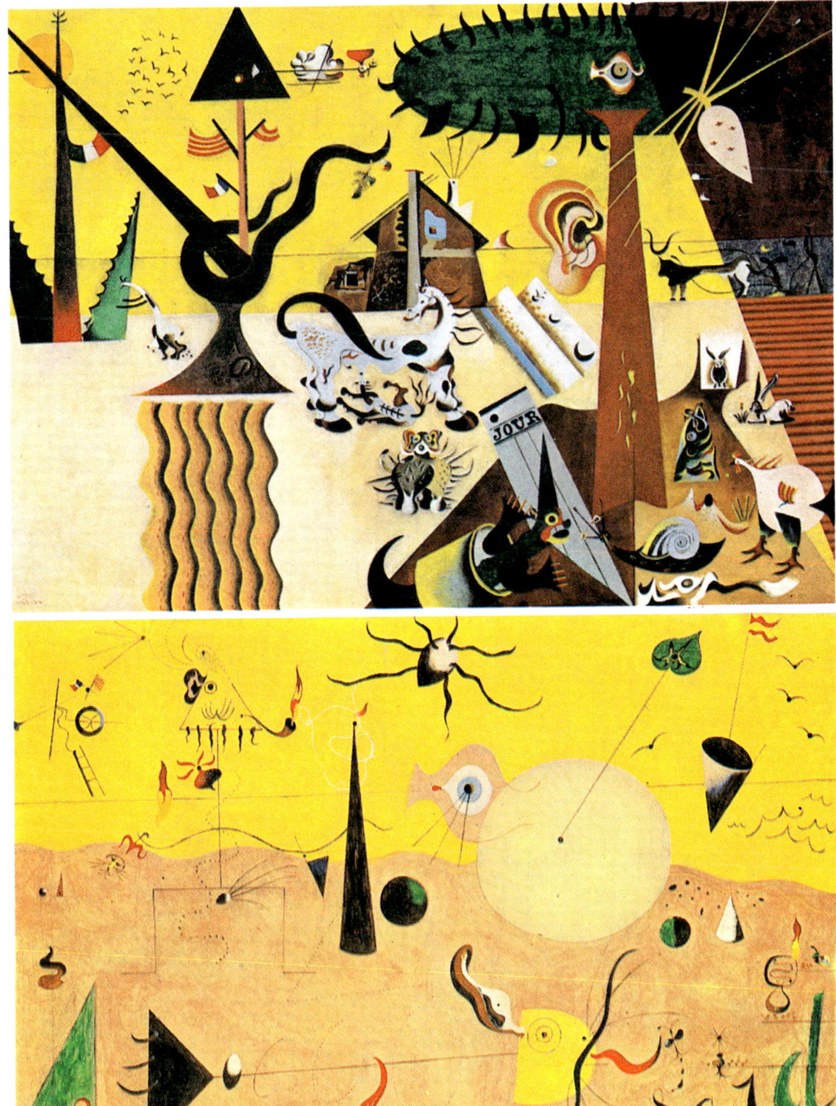

Top :
The Tilled Field
1923-1924

Bottom :
Catalan Landscape (The Hunter)
1923-1924

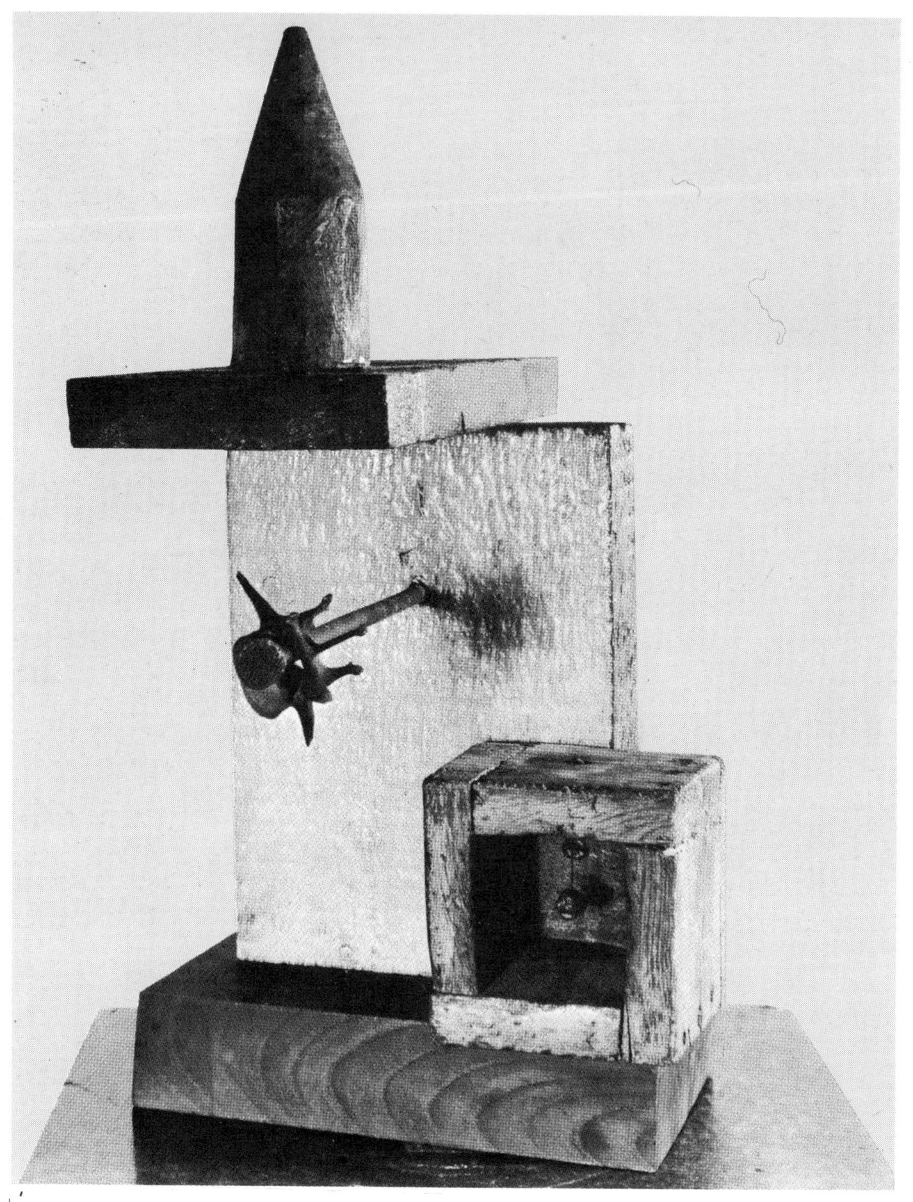

Object
1931

This said, there remains an inexplicable break (at least seen from today) between the pictures done in 1922-1923 and those done in 1923-1924, when Miró's Surrealist adventure proper began: *The Tilled Field*, *Pastoral*, *The Hermitage*, *The Family*, *The Trap*, *The Kiss*, and *Portrait of Madame K*. Concerning this matter, Jacques Dupin recalls that Miró had been in contact with the Dada movement since 1917, through the intermediary of Picabia and his Barcelona-based review *391*, and with Tristan Tzara since his move to Paris. Yet this does not entirely explain what Dupin calls the "turning point."

In *The Carbide Lamp*, Miró had attained not the utmost in realism, but its barest form, the transformation of an object into the harshest representation possible. Of course, the atmosphere on the Rue Blomet, full of unruly Surrealists, did contribute to the sudden transformation of Miró's seriousness into gaiety; and Miró may even have modified certain pictures he was then working on. But the poetic and formal innovation found in *The Tilled Field* cannot be directly linked to the boisterous spirit that reigned in the Surrealists' studios. It is as if Miró had decided, on his own, to tear down the fences on his *Farm* and set the animals free. The drawing of each detail suggests the quickness with which it was drawn; and even if there is somewhat of a tendency to solemnize the spontaneous series of sudden ideas, the brushwork shows a fundamental simplicity and boldness. A new quickness appeared in the conception of the artwork, and changed the process of its execution. Wandering between Paris and Montroig, Miró took advantage of the journey to stop placing things in direct relationship to each other. His associations are not those of contiguity, but of wandering.

Immediately realizing that *The Tilled Field* represented an irreversible leap, Miró wrote to a friend: "I have managed to escape into the absolute of nature, and my landscapes have nothing to do with the reality of the outside world." Even before he met Breton, his goal was taking shape: "to express all the golden sparks of our soul." To this end, he stuck a big ear on the trunk of the pine tree that dominates *The Tilled Field* and, in the foliage,

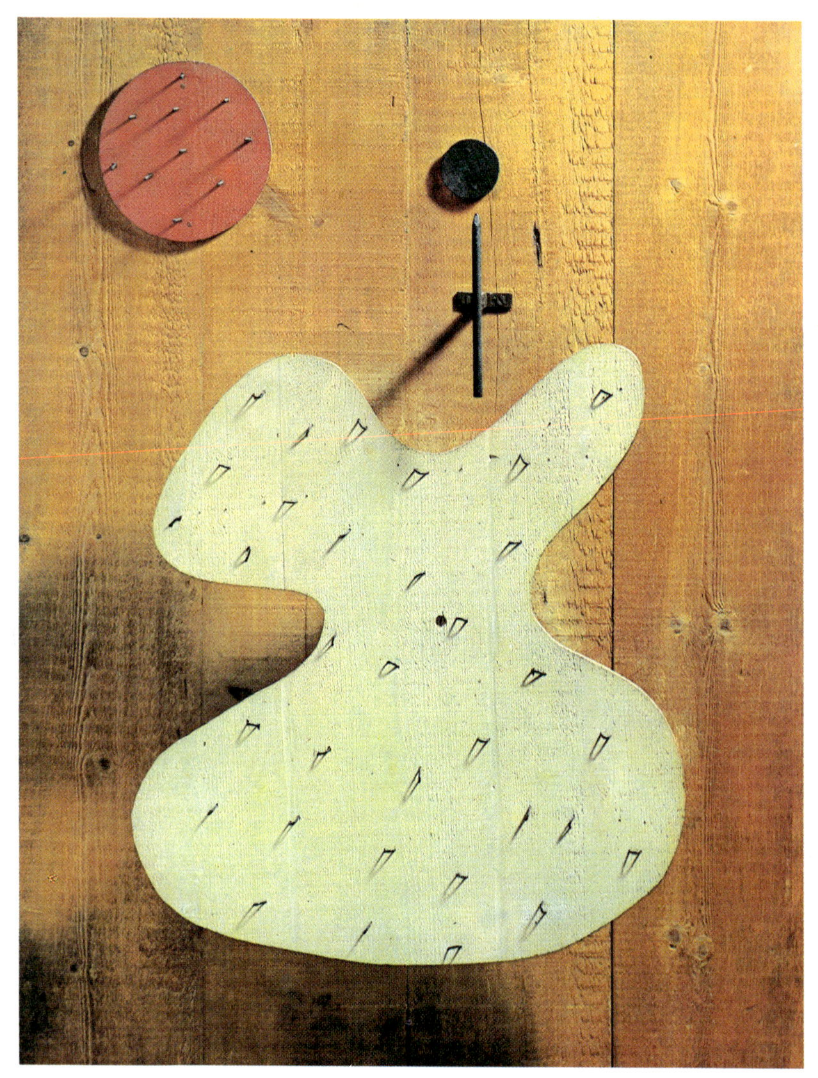

Construction
1930

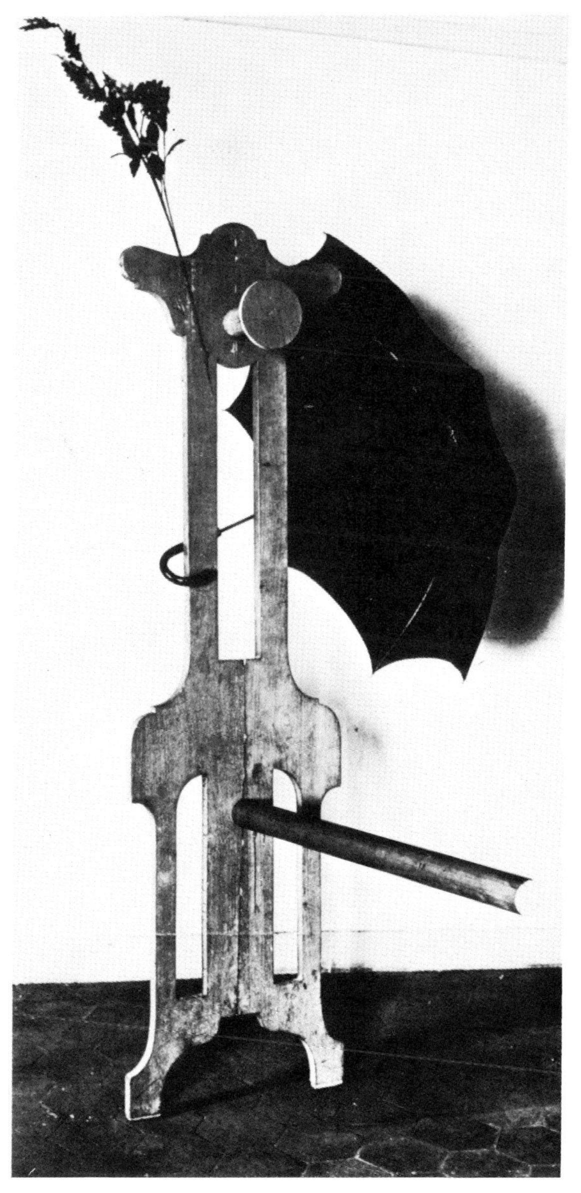

Personage with Umbrella
1931

painted a rainbow-lidded eye. After *The Tilled Field*, all of his pictures were to be made without a model, from drawings conceived at one go or from very rapid notations.

Where did these new forms come from ? From him, and him alone. In *The Hunter*, the sun is transformed into an eye watching the human figures and objects as they disobey all the rules of realism, changing not only in form, but also in scale, due to the simplification of the drawing. Dupin described this as a "reduction from object to line," which is true as far as it goes; but more than a reduction, there is a transformation of object into ideogram. Gone is the eternal conflict between drawing and painting. The pictures done in 1924 owe as much to drawing as they do to painting as if the automatism behind their conception had imposed a magical new figurative writing that transcended—by forgetting them—the problems the "chemist of intelligence" André Masson was still grappling with in the studio next door. By shifting symbolism towards the hidden meaning of the most everyday things, Giorgio de Chirico had changed the way men look at the world. A new murmur arose from the shadows in his sleepy squares; the door opened onto the unknown language that is ours when we dream. Miró went a step further and ascribed the signs of a new system of writing to objects, thus fusing painting and ideography.

"For me," he said, "a tree is not a tree, something belonging to the plant category, but something human, something alive. A tree has a personality of its own ... and can be quite disturbing! As you know, I sometimes stick an eye or an ear on trees. Trees can see and hear!" Refusing to speak *about* trees, he let them speak for themselves. He was to do the same for birds, stars, and objects. "The whole world is watching us," he also said, speaking about Romanesque frescoes, and the entire body has eyes. Miró showed not what the eye sees, but what the skin sees...

What can skin see? Shadows of cold, luminous heat, abyssal blacks, velvety greens and reds, infinite blues, fullness, emptiness, lines, boundaries between things, gropingly explored and recognized by the

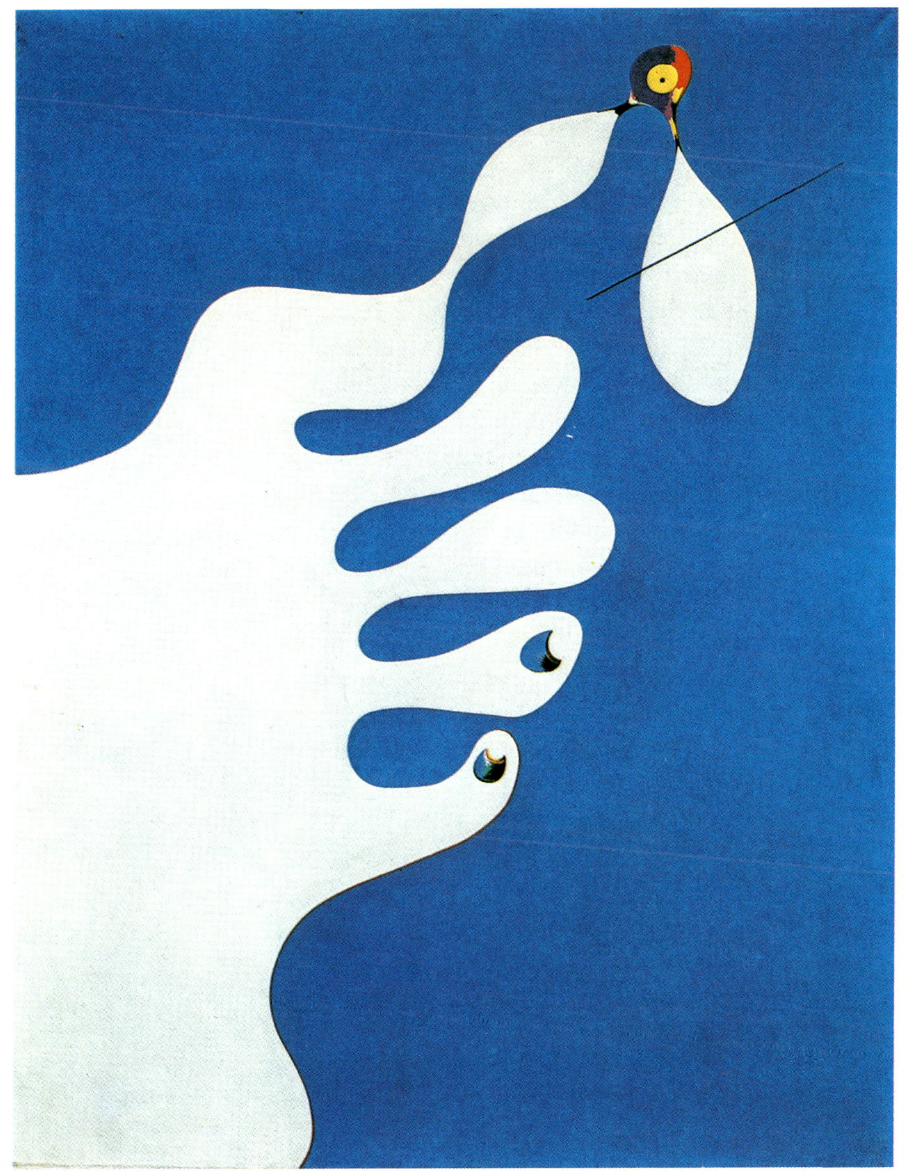

Hand Catching a Bird
1926

blind, linked together by the body's gestures and movements. Through automatic drawing, Miró entered an unnamed universe, our own, with the astonished indiscretion of a hand entering a glove: a hand that *sees*, little by little, the inside of the glove, adheres to it finger by finger, without knowing anything about its outer surface, the inaccessible, infinite limit. Miró entered our universe from beneath the visible.

Going from tightly framed barnyards or kitchens to the unframeable totality of nature—his "absolute"—and abandoning what has sometimes been called the "detailism" of his early realistic pictures, Miró arrived, in two years of Surrealism, at a kind of instinctive universalism where the All freely mingles with the Nothing, and not just dream with reality. To achieve this, he had to "link the unlinkable," but also to show that one does not necessarily have to establish links to feel the vacillating cohesion and dancing mutability—the permanent cataclysm—of the most distant, separate things. To do so, he had no need of symbols of union or god. The first lines that came to him sufficed: lines on a page like improvised footsteps in the sand, dots, commas, and musical phrases in the undulating crests of the sea, the memory signs of a man who has gone blind discovering the infinite richness of the visible world. For Miró, each thing detached itself and flew away from the others. Miró's favorite animal was the bird. As he drew, he composed a musical score of birdlike, birdy things. A graphic rather than phonetic cabbala, the bird language Miró invented leaves whoever looks at his pictures the greatest possible liberty of interpretation. Apart from a few poets, few have taken advantage of this liberty. Could it be that we do not know how to verbalize the unbounded liberty of signs that animates the universe?

"When I am working," he told Dora Vallier many years later, "I go into ecstasy. My painting overflows. I start a drawing and end up doing ten or fifteen! One leads to another; or rather, each drawing comes out of the precedent one!" In order to achieve this spontaneous proliferation, he had to free himself from the laws of gravity, from the heavy apparatus of representation, by ridding himself of his obsession with his native territory:

had he not taken the plunge and accepted the risk of poverty, Miró would never have become Miró. He had to experience the state of weightlessness one discovers in drifting and isolation, to suffer from hunger and even hunger-induced hallucinations (Miró always refused to ask his parents for money to survive on). The first inevitable consequences of Miró's move to Paris were a loss of self-confidence, self-doubts, and groping experimentation from one picture to the next between 1918 and 1923, five years of overly sober and prudent painting. He was walking a tightrope and struggling to keep his balance. He needed these five years to cut the umbilical cord attaching him to the investigations and experiences that were his as an adolescent, and to get rid of the classical subjects: landscapes, portraits, still lifes, pipes, newspapers, pedestal tables! Like a balloon released into the air, his painting suddenly soared in 1923. The accumulation found in the realistic canvases gave way to empty space, where it remained for him to invent what he called "the trajectory of mind over an entire lifetime, not what one has done during it, but what it gives a glimpse of and will allow others to do in the near or distant future..." Painting suddenly became an energetic exercise, an expenditure. It ceased to be a reflection of self and became a zooming arrow—ever more arrows shot at random into the night.

In 1923, Masson advised Miró to stop by a Montparnasse gallery on the corner of the Rue Vavin and the Rue Notre-Dame-des-Champs, where there was an exhibition of pictures by a complete unknown: Paul Klee. It is not known which of Klee's pictures were on display, but Miró liked them. They would seem to have triggered an abrupt change in his way of painting. But the pictures Miró painted in 1923-1924 are not imitations of Klee. Similarly, in and after 1924, Miró did not apply the theory of automatism Breton formulated that year in his manifesto. It was in his own body and movements that he discovered how drawing could be linked to gesture. Breton could do nothing but take note of this after the fact; and when Benjamin Péret—and not Breton—wrote the preface for his exhibition at Pierre Loeb's gallery ("Les cheveux dans les yeux"), a Surrealist poet joined him, for the first time, in the space he had liberated. Klee's pictures allowed him to feel,

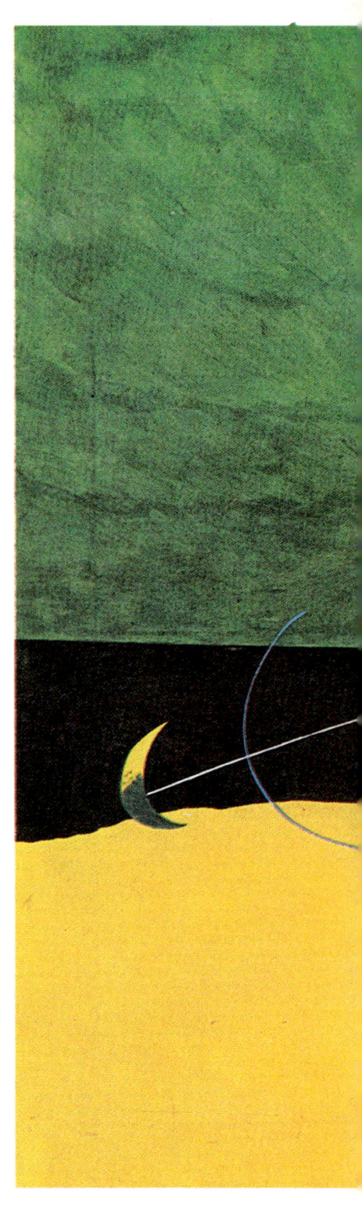

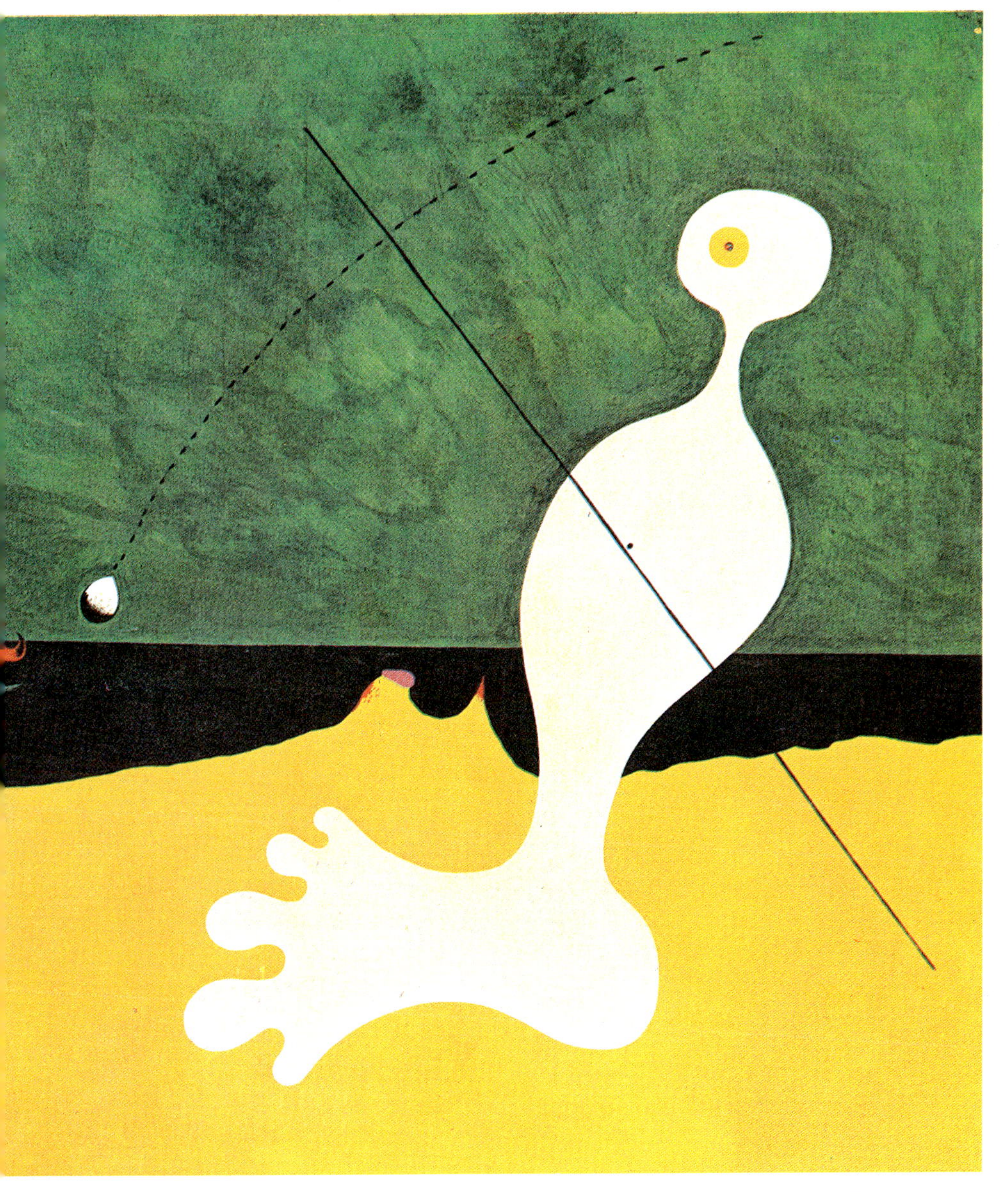

Person Throwing a Stone at a Bird
1926

he once remarked, "that there was more to visual expression than painterly painting, that it was necessary to go beyond it, to reach deeper, more moving zones."

More Surrealistic than the Surrealists, or a Surrealist before the fact, Miró was ahead of them in the evolution that would later lead, via Duchamp and Matta, to the search for a larger cosmogony than that of dreaming and dream illustrations. Doubtless, he was too far ahead for Breton to realize it, too quiet and discreet under his rock, untouched by all the manifestoes and rhetoric, for Breton (ultra-sensitive to hidden voices, but deaf to the music of silence) to hear him clearly. Between 1924 and 1928, Breton was as unprepared as everybody else, which did not, however, keep him from realizing that Miró had entered Surrealism like a tree branch suddenly blowing in through the window.

When Miró embarked on the series of "dream paintings," he ventured into uncharted territory. He was no longer trying to prove to his father that he was a painter. His unconscious was no longer Oedipal: exit the family romance. Miró became a blank, an absolute blank, like someone floating on his back, far from the ocean shore, who sees nothing but sky—gray, blue, or white—hovering above. These monochrome paintings with cloudy backgrounds are mental gaps, skylights opening onto absence, a mental void. Nothing inhabits them: Miró had forced the phantoms out of his memory. Miró's dreams, which he claimed to have not at night, but in broad daylight as he worked, emptied him and his work of daily reality and social hostility. He painted these dreams in Paris, saving other subjects of a less uprooted nature, and more loaded with concrete meaning, for his summer stays in Montroig.

The hundred or so untitled "dream paintings" (most of the titles that have been given are wrong) reveal a desire to break radically with everything: to slam the door on the theatre of painting, avant-gardes, and social relations. They are a kind of mental exile. Michel Leiris, who saw them in the Rue Blomet studio, compared them to "faded walls on which generations of

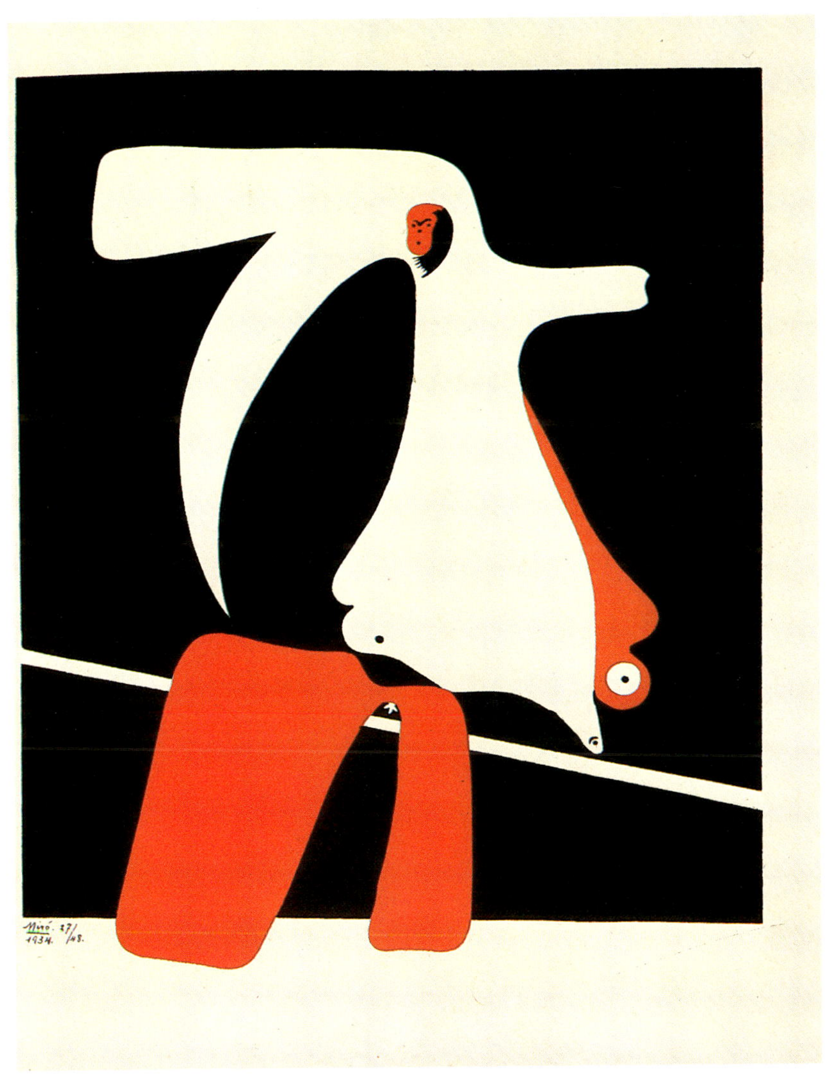

Lithograph
1934

billstickers, aided by centuries of drizzle, have inscribed mysterious poems, long stains with cloudy, blurred shapes like alluvial deposits from who knows where, sand carried along by rivers constantly changing course, subjected as they are to the motion of wind and rain." It is as if Miró had started painting with his eyes closed, in order to enter, in the backgrounds of these paintings without backgrounds, the vastness of infinity—where the infinitely small dwells and men become prisoners struggling in their mazes. He did not project himself into these paintings, nor record his phantasms in them, except for a few signs—a red glide, a white ball, a black or white star, a vague head—zooming like little flares through what René Gaffé has called an "aerial ocean." The destiny of Nothing.

Thirty years ahead of the postwar American painters (including Sam Francis) and the allover, Miró invented a new space. It does not drown the viewer, but forces him to leave self behind. We cross through appearances, which are destroyed in the crossing, but the crossing leads nowhere. There are no gods on the other side—no heaven and no hell. We are in the vacant space that separates each of us from everyone else. Still not talking when he did these paintings, Miró gave pictorial form to his silence—not to the silence that was his among his talkative frieds at the Brasserie Cyrano, but to the silence he sank into alone in his studio. He thus revealed the vastness that separated him from himself and kept him from realizing what was happening within him. Never did he devote so many pictures to a single theme, or rather to a single absence of theme; and it was toward this void that his pictures hurled him.

On a ground where the few remaining forms are stray soundings, only poems could be inscribed: *My brunette's body because I love her like a cat dressed in lettuce green like hail it's one and the same*, to give one example, is simply a kind of waking thought or automatic haiku. For, automatic poems, as anyone who has actually read any knows, could be said to be deprived of concepts. They are frenzies of love or rage, dreamed encounters, the opposite of philosophical discourse or literary analysis—which is why they have received so little attention. Readers do

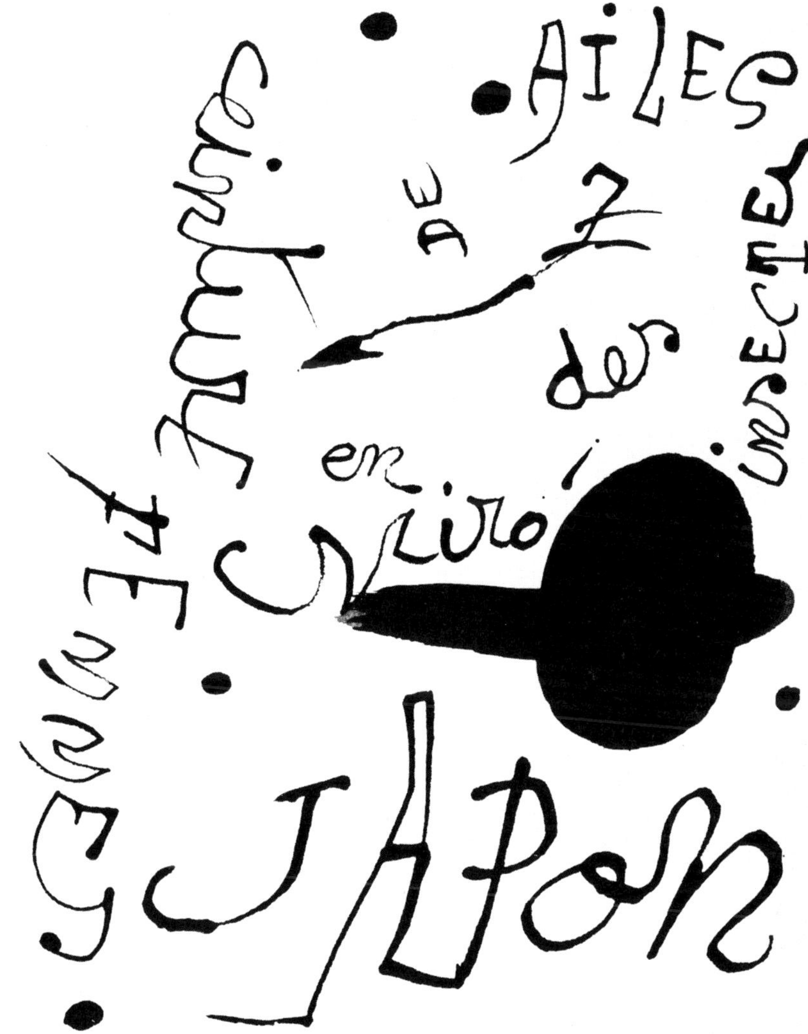

Drawing-poem
1976

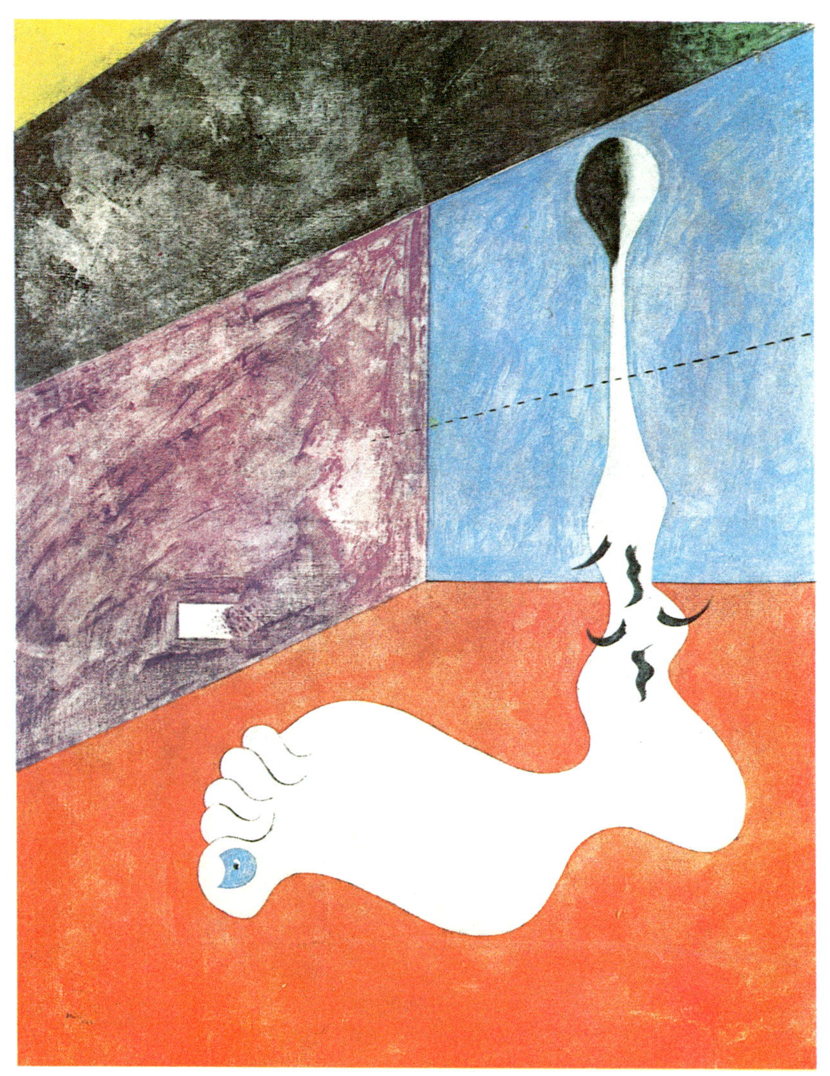

The Statue
1925

not find their own ideas and clichés in automatic poetry; they prefer slowly flowing rivers to these cascades. Miró's automatic sentences, like those in the poetry of Jean Arp, Péret, Aragon, Breton, or Picasso, escaped from his mouth as if he were breathing out words. Without beginning or end, they lead nowhere, if not to derision, answer the enigmas they create with other enigmas, and give the slip to all forms of discursive reasoning and all theories. The individual practice of verbal automatism results in the negation of the theory that triggered it. One does not discover the "way thinking really works"; one submits to it and "subjectivizes" it. Similarly, "dream painting" results in the creation of a personal space. One does not "dream" while painting anymore than while writing. One is dreamed. Surrealism, by subjectivizing itself, broke loose from its moorings with everything.

It is as if, in 1925, painting, the assassination of which Miró had not yet called for, slipped through his fingers and vanished into thin air. He saw it as something foreign to himself, the way a murderer sees his corpse. How did the crime happen? Some unexpected blast of energy derailed the machine; an inner hand knocked down the ladder to the sky. Stunned senseless by something that has no name, Miró did not try to reconstruct a record of what had happened. The "dream paintings" were Miró's *tabula rasa*. "I do not think, therefore I paint" was his *cogito*. And yet, he was thinking...

What about? The pictures Miró painted before leaping into the void were too rich, loaded with symbols, and thematically close to his psychological make-up for him not to have contemplated getting as far away as possible from them. In 1924 and 1925, indeed, Miró had painted a series of very inventive ironical pictures, the most famous of which is *The Harlequin's Carnival*. In the same vein, he had treated *The Family* in a less-known work and woman in the highly symbolic *Portrait of Madame K*. All of these pictures—and lighter works such as *Le Renversement* and *Maternity* do not contradict this—are tied to the idea of collective play, celebration, and disguise. It is as if, in order to break with his past, Miró needed first to put

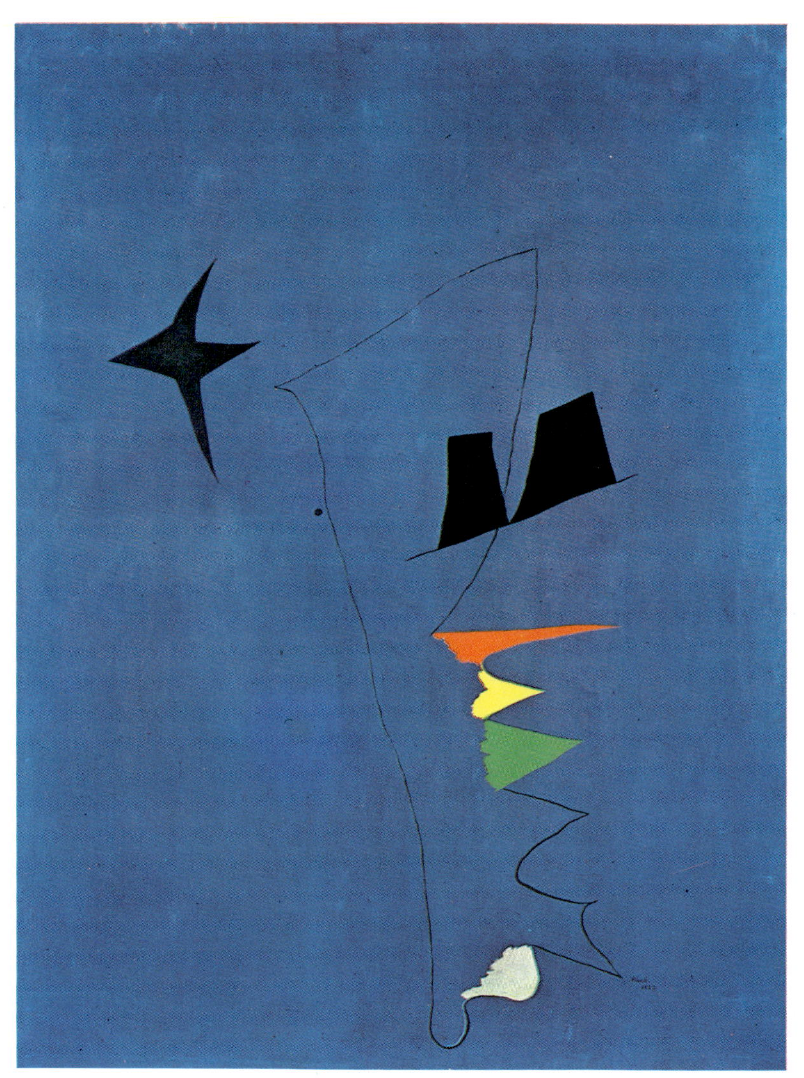

Blue Ground
1927

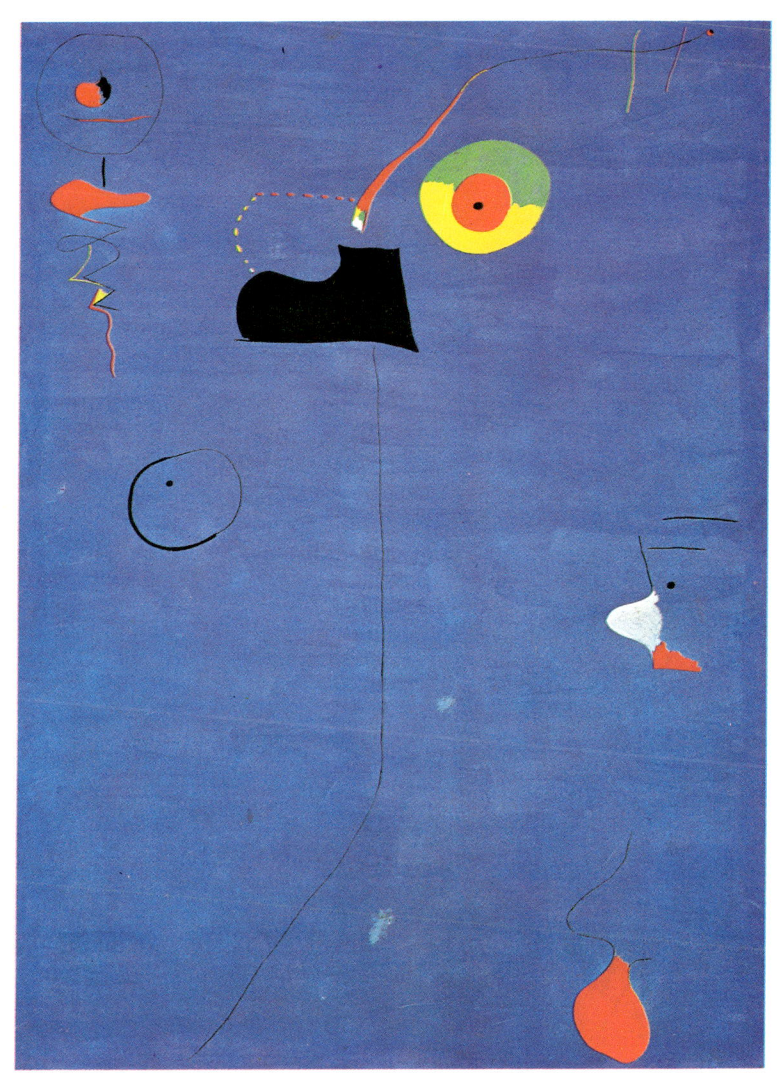

Three Figures (Fratellini)
1927

on a show by transforming men and women into mannequins, automatons, or actors in a comic opera. (Miró loved to dress up. For the private view of his exhibition at Pierre Loeb's, he had, in spite of his poverty, put together a special outfit: an embroidered jacket, gray trousers and white gaiters.) Presiding over this metamorphosis was the Harlequin, who—another irony—is a Catalan peasant.

Miró's derision spared nothing, least of all the family, presented as if on a stage, with the big voyeur's eye watching through the window. This was a way of telling his Surrealist friends: "Even if I never speak, I am just as capable of defying society as you are; but the best way for me to scandalize is with my pictures". In his suit of many colors, the Harlequin is also man clothed in the patchwork of society. Shown with her attributes—the L-square, the triangle, the bird-stem, the flames and roots of the heart—Madame K. becomes nothing but an anonymous model, stripped of all Chirico-like mystery, a kind of artificial construction that depersonalizes femininity. The skeleton of things and beings has shrunk to the symbols that evoke them. Anguish is conjured away.

Using humor and self-mockery to reveal that he was not the innocent others took him for, Miró freed himself from his seriousness through parody. But the celebration he put on left him with that emptiness one feels when the party's over. He had successfully played a role he was not meant to play. He was living in an epoch of Harlequins; but he wanted to go farther, to soar beyond his epoch and experience time as an "end of the world," the title of one of his most beautiful paintings, done in 1925, before inventing another form of humor, outlined that same year in *The Statue*'s single, enormous foot of a bodiless man with a minuscule, faceless head. This new humor was not intended to provoke laughter, but to disconcert or shock—to trip the viewer up. With *Person Throwing a Stone at a Bird*, this new kind of humor entered the history of painting.

In that picture, the same foot as in *The Statue*, the foot of a man whose head replaces his knee, is shown throwing a stone at a bird that resembles a

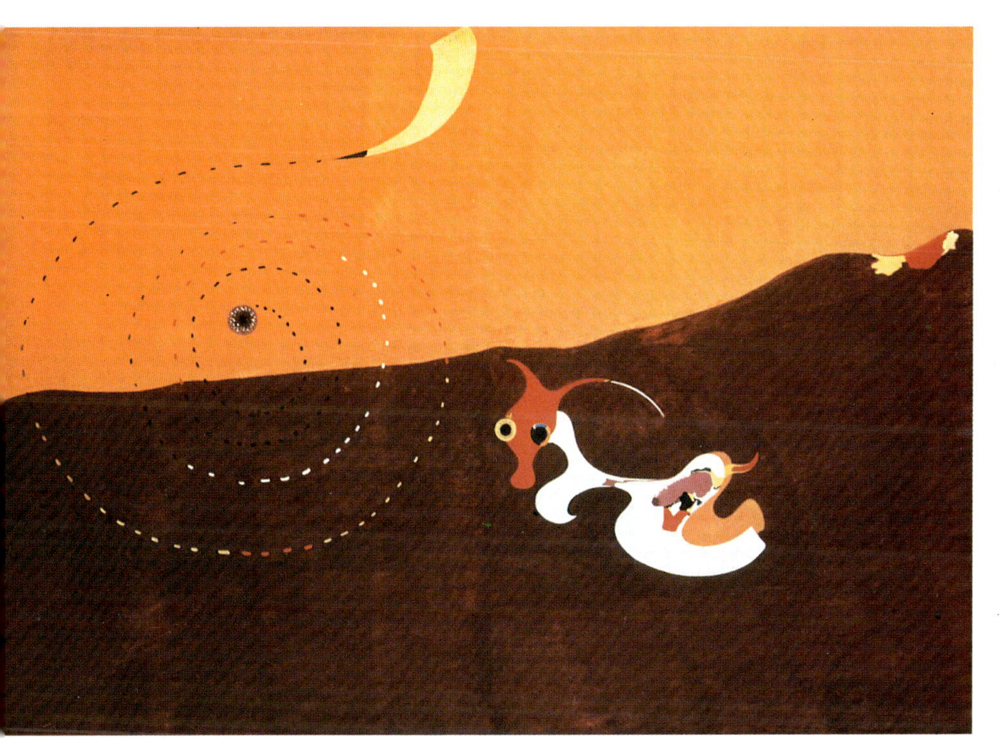

Landscape known as The Hare
1927

bow and arrow—with a red-crested head at one end of the shaft, a crescent moon at the other—in a tricolored landscape of yellow, black, and green, where the sky is green, the sea black. Unlike Masson, the stuff of whose ecstasies was tragedy, Nietzsche and the atrocities of trench warfare, Miró sought to forget through lightness. This lightness has the beauty created when an image is detached from all discursive reasoning and all mythologies. When Miró painted this picture in 1926, he had already been through his experience of the void; he was living in a deserted landscape. The field of the picture is occupied by the single idea of throwing a stone at a bird. Around the foot-man, the outline of a bow and arrow reduplicates the shape of the bird. The picture is a derision of the human claim to be superior to animals and the strong's claim to be superior to the weak, a derision of combat. The man's arms are reduced to a straight line, the bird's wings to a curve. There is no theatrical illusion; the paint starts talking by itself. But this is not a painterly painting. Miró invented a kind of poetic painting—without references, without literature, beyond interpretation. Liberated from the context of words, an idea becomes weightless. It soars into flight. Miró set painting free to fly in the sky of ideas. Like the pre-Socratics, before philosophy was transformed into a school, he learned to see and think without blinders.

At the same time, he began to enjoy life. When Georges Raillard tried to get the painter to admit that women upset, frightened, and horrified him, he did not succeed. Miró, who out of politeness had not dared to contradict his questioner, put an end to the discussion (*Ceci est la couleur de mes rêves*). For once, the artist who always agreed with whatever interpretations it pleased the critics to give his work (even when he knew he was leading them astray) did not answer "that's right." To settle the question, all he needed to say was: "For me, the female sex is like the planets and shooting stars. *It's a part of my vocabulary.*" Miró's birds are not alone. The image of the vulva freely frolics through his paintings like a will-o'-the-wisp.

The spontaneously drawn, freely circulating forms, the gratuitous intersections, the lively choreography of colors, sexes, birds, and

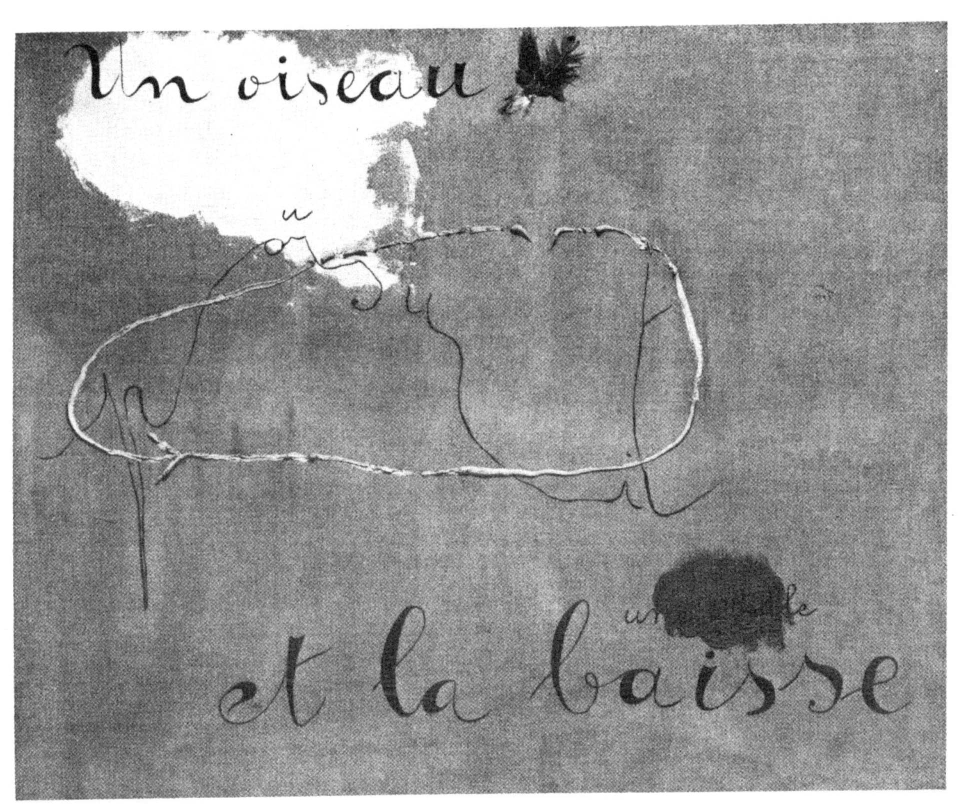

A Bird Chases a Butterfly and Lowers It
1927

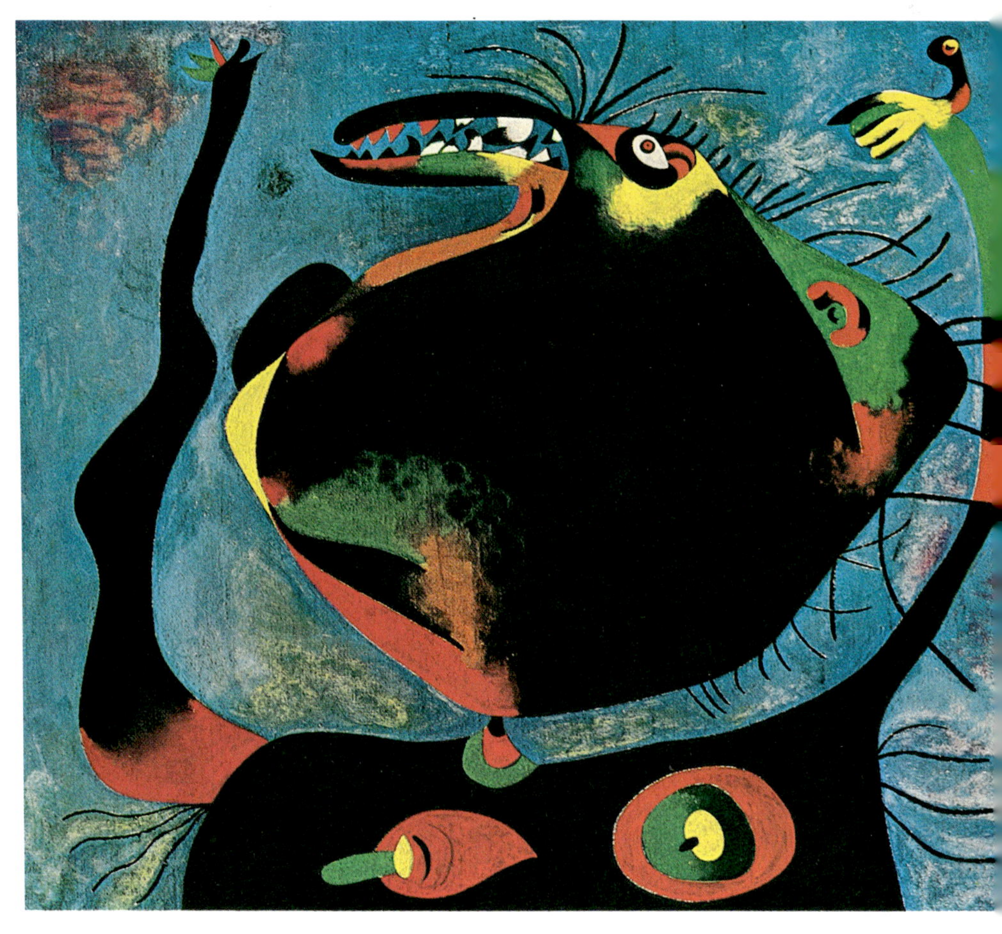

Woman's Head
1938

women—everything that makes up Miró's "vocabulary" escapes the grasp of the sadness and pomp found in the highly rhetorical works of all other 20th-century painters except Duchamp and Klee. Miró's mocking, tender nimbleness, which has so often been misunderstood by the critics (including Malraux, who spoke a bit too quickly of Miró's "imps"), as well as his pleasure in gaily painting the aerobatic adventure of things human, might also be explained as a deflation of man's, or rather male, omnipotence. In his pictures, the male genitals are depicted rarely or—when they are shown, as in the 1924 canvas *The Trap*—comically.

Could it be that speech is synonomous with male autocracy? Miró could only bear the words of the poets, for they are not overburdened with seriousness and do not make a display of knowledge. Contrary to what Margit Rowell says in her original study of Miró's poetry-painting, in which she lucidly compares his large mural paintings to anonymous wordless poems, Miró never literally illustrated a single poem, no more than he ever copied or imitated a single painting. He could playfully capture the underlying idea, but refused to adhere strictly to the work, as I realized when he "illustrated" my *Liberté des libertés*.

In one of his pictures from 1926, Miró wrote: *Un oiseau poursuit une abeille et la baisse* (A bird chases a bee and lowers it); and it is true that Robert Desnos had written in the group of poem-puns found in *L'Aumonyme*:

ser
des cils a bai
ssé
(eyelashes to kiss lowered)

Miró had agreed to illustrate these poems in the volume *Désordre formel*, which was scheduled to come out in 1929, but never existed as such. Margit Rowell may not have known about this, but it does strengthen her hypothesis that Miró had intentionally written *baisse* instead of *baise*.

Personally, I would tend to agree with Dupin that we are dealing with one of those spelling mistakes the Catalan painter sometimes made in French—which is not to say that this might not be an unconscious poetic slip. But Miró never consciously quoted from his knowledge. He always had the daring to paint as if he knew nothing. Indeed, he was so suspicious of the cleverness that comes with talent—he even reproached Picasso for this—that he strove to thwart it. Everything he detested in Breton's "brilliance," as well as his distrust of all dogmatic thought, is, moreover, linked to his distrust of displays of virility. In his pictures, he never stopped mocking virile pretension. In his famous *Bullfight*, he even went so far as to ridicule the archetype of virility: the greatest macho show-off of them all, the matador himself.

The weakness of the strong lies, above all, in their dread of death. Miró subtly suggested to Raillard that Picasso feared death more than anything. "Picasso spoke about this openly with Jacqueline, who told me: 'He's very worried. Death is a phantom he cannot shake.' But this had nothing to do with religion. It was the idea of dying that worried him in a very Spanish way. Not Catalan, Spanish! Personally, I don't give a darn about it! It doesn't worry me in the slightest! I don't even think about it! It's just too bad, you know!" Miró-the-Catalan-painter-of-women-vulvas-birds-and-stars here traced the boundary separating him from the virile-Spanish-painter-of-bulls. General Franco, whom Miró once compared to Père Ubu, was for him the most grotesque caricature of Spanish virility. Everything he invented and introduced into his "vocabulary" defies death and, as it floats through the vulva-dotted sky, bids farewell to those who fear it. When Raillard reminded him that he had once said his dying words would be "to hell with it," Miró, true to the spirit of revolt of his youth, joyously exclaimed: "To hell with society! To hell with all of society! To hell with everything unimportant!" Behind Miró's insolent gaiety lay a "To hell with men!" and, under that, a "To hell with God!" This is how his bird "lowering" and "kissing" the bee is to be understood, not as a borrowing from Desnos! The bird is a "part of his vocabulary"! The bee is *not*!

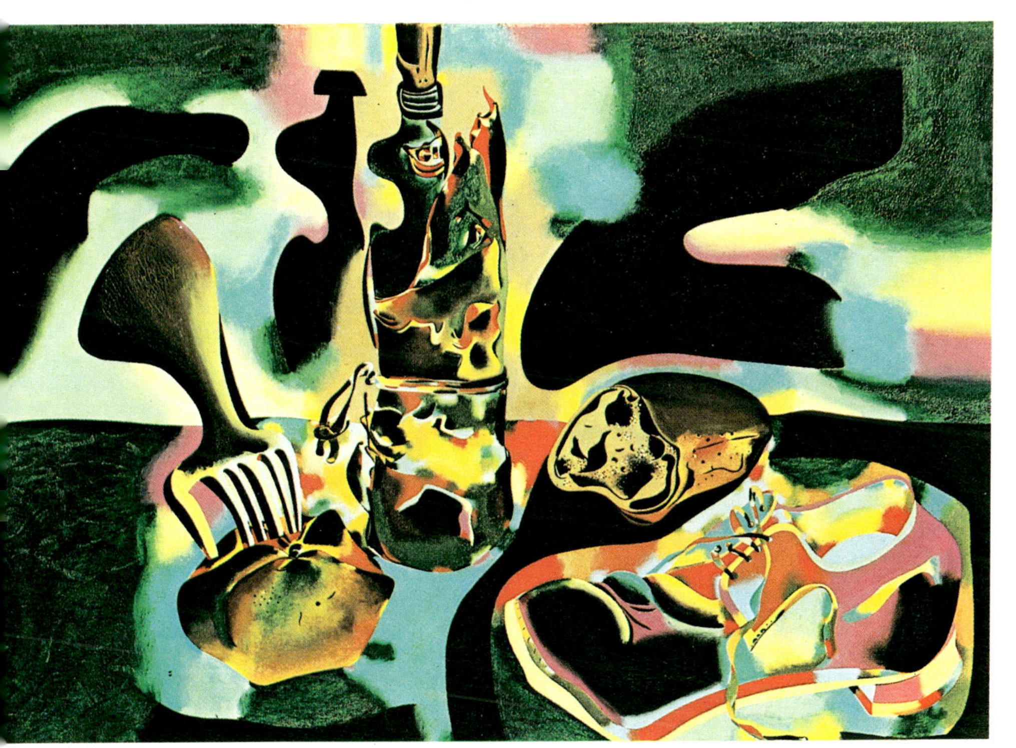

Still Life with Old Shoe
1937

Screaming and alive, the magnificent *Woman's Head* Miró painted in 1938, as the Spanish Civil War raged on, proclaims that "liberty is a woman" much more directly—in a more emotional and intimate way—than *Guernica*, which is an "historical painting" in the sense that Jacques-Louis David and his students gave that term. He had, of course, first painted the cry of popular revolt seen in *The Reaper* (or "Catalan Peasant in Revolt") for the pavilion of the Spanish Republic at the 1937 Paris World's Fair, where *Guernica* was also exhibited. But, like an afterthought brought on by the bad turn the civil war was taking for the Republicans, Miró's revolt against authority attained its greatest power of persuasion in *Woman's Head*: a poetic power that he desperately opposed to political power. In comparison, his 1932 *Man's Head* seems empty and abstract: a purely formal exercise, easy the way painterly paintings can be.

During the 1930s, Miró, like all of the other Surrealists, was haunted by sinister spectres that, try as he might, he could not chase away. They provided the matter of the investigations that would lead, in 1940, to the "Constellations," which were foreshadowed by two tapestry cartoons done in 1934: *Snail Woman Flower Star*, in which the woman coordinates the free interplay of words and forms as if she were, for Miró, painting itself, and *Swallow Love*, in which the title words seem to have been written on the canvas by the figures in the picture. Not even the Cubists had so perfectly integrated writing and painting. In the overloaded context of the 1930s, these two works are exceptional. They came five years before *A Dewdrop Falling from a Bird's Wing Awakens Rosalie Sleeping in the Shade of a Spider's Web*, the "rosace" that Miró painted in 1939 in Varengeville, on the eve of the "Constellations." But it is interesting to note that the role of forerunner was played by "tapestry cartoons," as if Miró were never more intuitive and incisive than when working in a minor key.

From his beginnings up to the end, Miró's greatness resulted from the poetic and plastic amplification of everything small (birds, dragonflies, dewdrops, stars twinkling from afar) or on the fringes of "important things" such as history's great men and their heroic acts. Like a poet who sees a

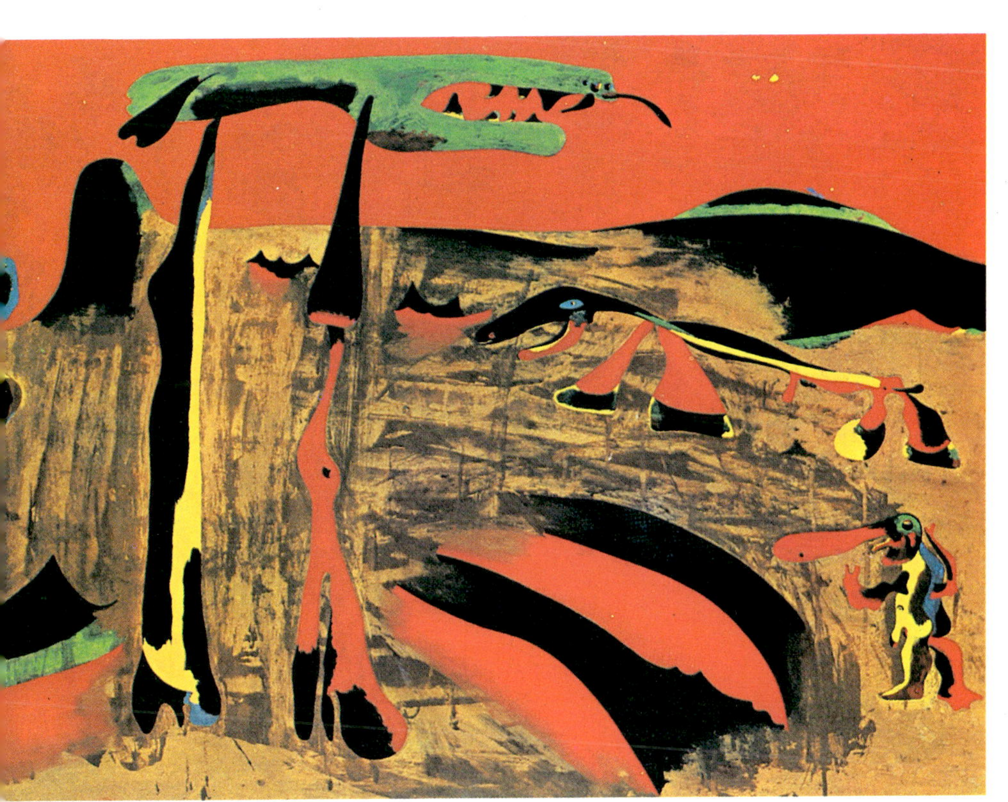

Figures in Nature
1935

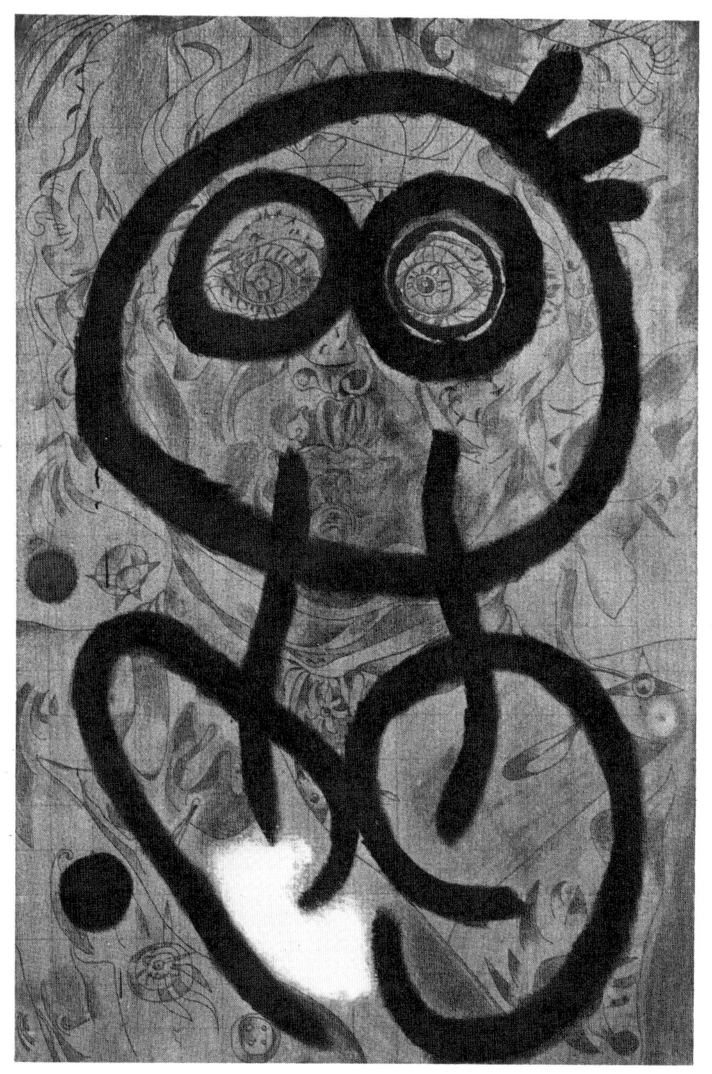

Self Portrait
1937-1960

little girl as greater than the entire universe, he accorded the same importance to the minor genres of engraving and lithography as he did to his paintings. He could do nothing without saying the opposite of those who, thinking themselves stronger than everyone else, confiscate the very idea of power before actually saying or doing anything at all. But he did not merely speak out; he *showed* his opposition. And he not only showed it; he took pleasure in showing it. He knew he was right because he had fun working and was never ashamed. For Miró, beauty was not a matter of magnifying a preexisting power, but of *bringing the vastness of the universe, the power to represent the infinitely large to the infinitely small.* All of his efforts, so coherent, can be explained in terms of the need he had felt since childhood: to make everything that is small and apparently unessential, gratuitous, and unjustifiable from an aesthetic or political point of view the real *subject* of all revolutionary painting.

Someone once said that, unlike Picasso, Miró never confused painting with keeping a diary. The remark has weathered the years. Whoever it was who made it may have been forgetting that fiction—or invention—is only an indirect, but transparent, way of saying or showing the unjustifiable truth about oneself. The myth of a childish, or even infantile, Miró stems from this universal oversight. Whenever someone creates something, he "cheats." The "realist" painters' sleight-of-hand consists in making us think they cheat less than other artists. In fact, like all the Surrealists, but in a more innocent way, Miró understood their trickery, just as he grasped the dishonest intentions of the abstract painters. Like a woman (Surrealism was in this sense feminine), he painted (making fun of himself and men, but never of women) the unfathomable, unexplorable truth of the *in-between*. The psychological geography of Miró's paintings is rooted in an underlying certainty that subverts the arrogant brand of painting, practiced by such artists as Picasso and Léger, in which intellectuals can easily read the ostentatious display of figures as confirmation of their various and sundry ideologies. In comparison with these "great painters," Miró remained on the fringes, but was never neutral. Politically, he was on the same side as the others, but did not proclaim his commitment to everybody and his brother.

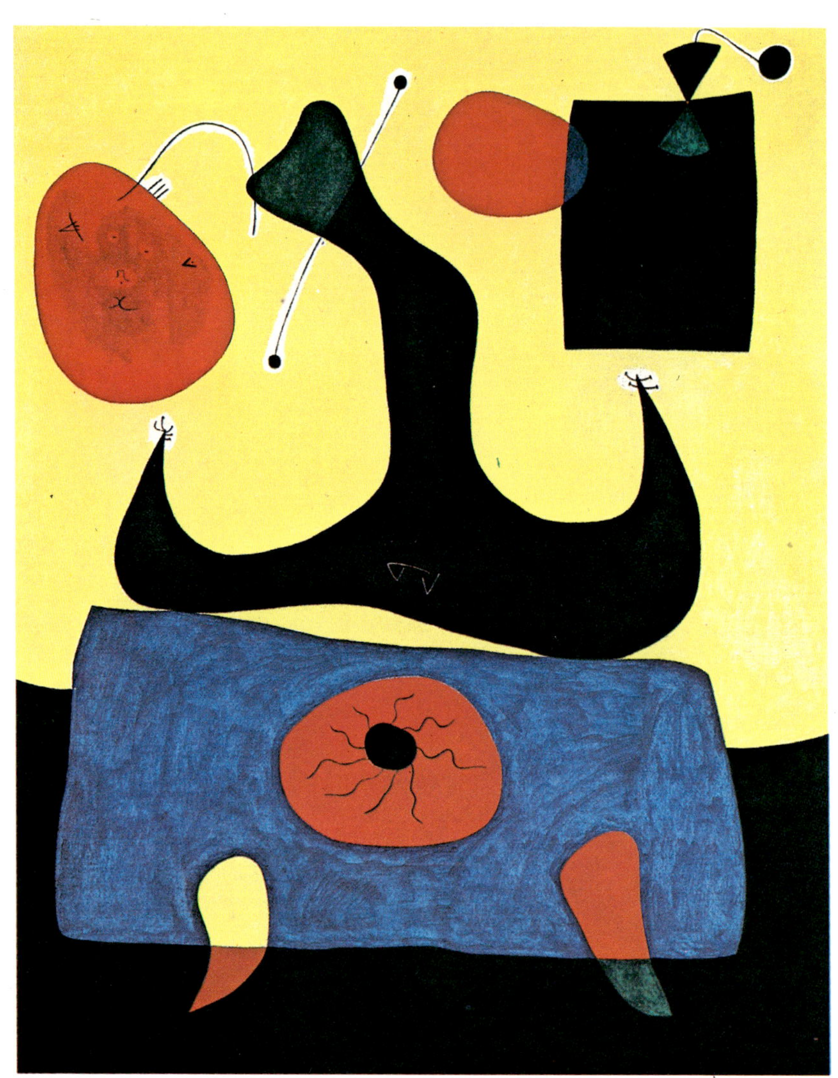

Seated Woman I
1938

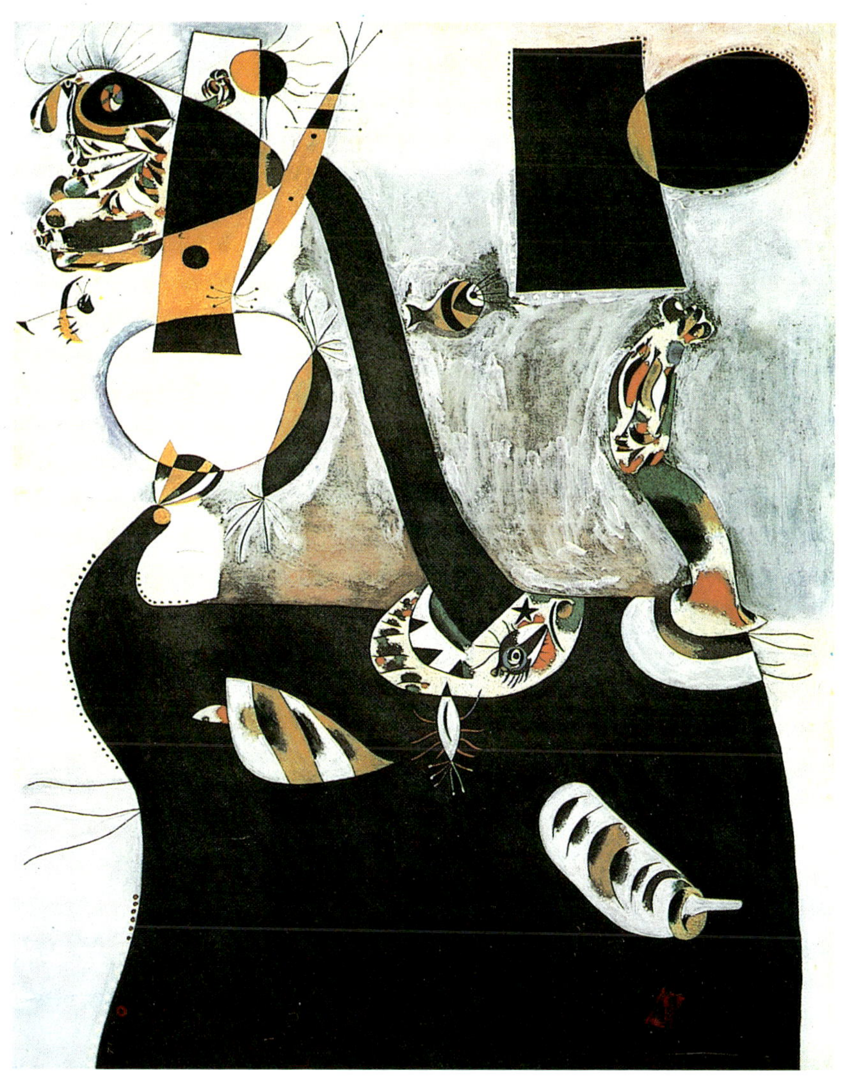

Seated Woman II
1939

Miró was naive the way silent painters are. By using new and incongruous or unexpected images, they hope to change the ideas of those they cannot find the words to answer in real life. Miró's zigzagging investigations in the 1930s and the inner contradictions he was going through, which led to such different pictures as *Forms on a Black Ground* and *Animated Landscape* (1935), can be understood only in terms of everyday problems communicating, which could not be solved using plastic means.

Miró may well have suffered more than others from misunderstandings brought on by exasperation and worrying. In 1932, Aragon broke with the Surrealists to side with the Communist Party for good. But nothing had prepared the poets and painters—who had dreamed in 1924 of a "new declaration of the rights of man" and a revolution more like that of 1789 than like the one in Leningrad in 1917—for the threat of extermination represented by the rise of Nazism and the strengthening of Stalinism. A certain number of artistic and intellectual aberrations thus ensued. Painters and poets—even the geniuses—are not seers. When they begin to stammer, it is because history is losing the power to speak rationally. Miró's paintings from the 1930s were responses to the pressures assailing him from all sides as he tried to keep his independence. Picasso and Léger were gesticulating with effectiveness and power. They were sure of themselves. But Marcel Duchamp had already been silent for many years. Among these very different individuals, Miró was not yet "somebody"; and if he was constantly trying to find new forms and orient his work in a new way, it is because he was sure of nothing.

Miró's anxiety over the political situation and bitter return to a feeling of social responsibility led him to realism. "In 1935," he once declared, "I was still showing space and forms in relief. There was still chiaroscuro in my painting; but, little by little, all of that disappeared. Around 1940, relief and chiaroscuro were suppressed altogether... Without relief or chiaroscuro, depth becomes limitless. Movement can spread out into infinity." The figures represented in his 1934 pastels, such as *The Opera Singer*, have a rather heavy or contorted sculptural quality about them. The 1934-1935 "paintings and painting-collages on sandpaper," an attempt to flatten the figures back out by emphasizing their silhouettes, range from simple graphic patterns (*Forms on a Black Ground*) to extremely powerful imaginary landscapes (*Figures in Nature*). In 1935, when Miró began modeling with greater relief and using more chiaroscuro, he also put new emphasis on the corporeal presence of his highly "inventive" figures and objects in pictures painted on masonite, such as *Figures Attracted by the Forms of a Mountain*, *Figures in Front of a Metamorphosis*, and *Man and Woman in Front of a Pile of Excrement*. In these paintings, the light, shade, and color produce a spectacular sense of the real. While he also continued painting highly simplified signs and figures—spots, dots, lines—up to 1937-1938, he realized his masterpiece of modeling and chiaroscuro in *Still Life with Old Shoe*, a work which, though an exception in his output, led some to think the painter was yielding to "tragic realism."

What saved him from repeating hackneyed aesthetic formulas, and from the illusion of a collective language, was his desire to experiment. Not only did he paint on masonite, copper, and sandpaper, but also on celotex, tarpaper, and brick; he realized painting-objects in which he inscribed signs on variously shaped scraps of wood glued to canvas, and even on a carob log in his 1938 *Object of Sunset* (which also includes a mattress spring and gas burner), which was long enthroned in the middle of André Breton's studio and now belongs to the Musée national d'art moderne in Paris. Experimentation was all the more necessary for him because his works were losing their center of gravity. Twisted, bloated, or split open by pain and suffering—as in the 1938 works *Woman's Head* and *Seated Woman*—the forms in these paintings are writhing as if they had been born in the agony of death. Miró had not lost his grace, but we can feel him doubting everything he did, backtracking, starting over, and stamping his feet in rage, never satisfied with his personal responses to the crises raging around him.

In spite of these contradictions and clashes, Miró was not led astray. He

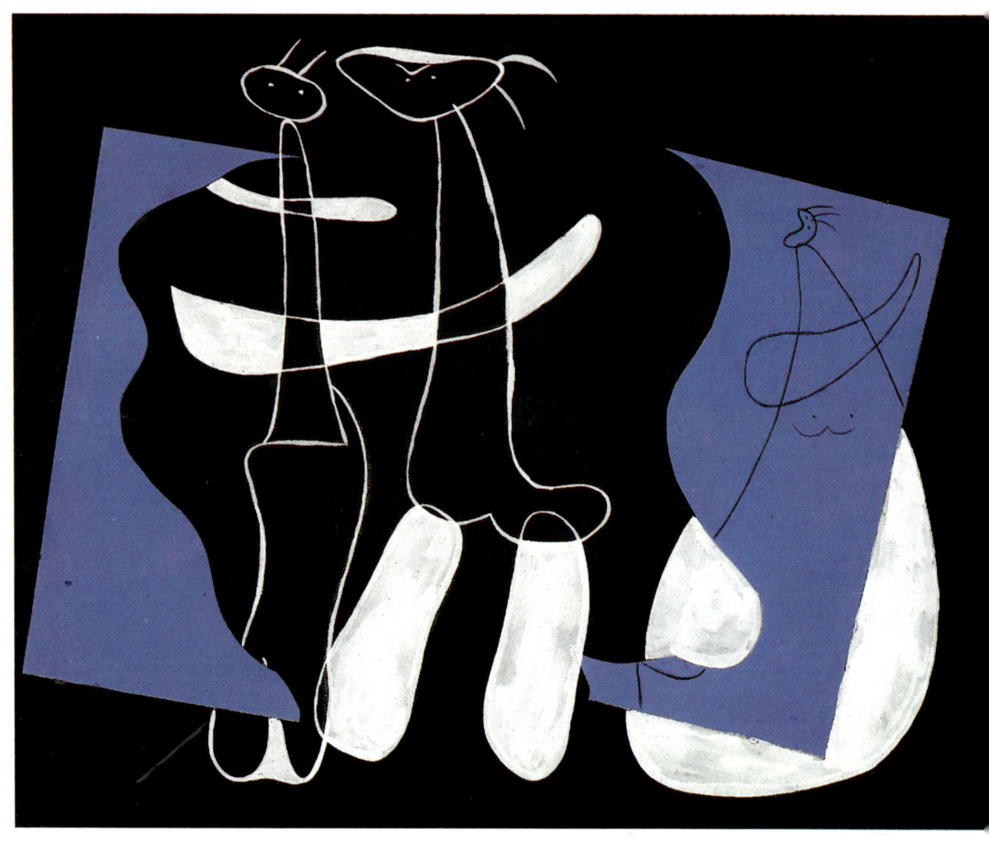

Three Figures on a Black Ground
1934

continued to paint to create a "balance," which was not a renaissance or a "return" to Classicism (Miró never felt anything but scorn for Dali), even less a side-stepping of the reality, conflicts, and hazards of his time, but rather a quite Surrealistic way of getting his mind to produce something other than complacent, repetitive ideas and beings. Something about painting itself always disturbed him: a heavy pathos which compelled him, but which he also always tried to escape—to become one with the liberty of the bird flying freely through the air.

Paradoxically enough, he was ready to do so in 1939, the year that war was declared. Dated September 8, 1939, seven days after the declaration of war, *Figures Magnetised by the Stars Walking on the Music of a Furrowed Landscape*, along with the nine or ten other small pictures he painted from August to December of the same year, announces not only the 1940-1941 series of "Constellations," but also the splendid heights his work would attain after the defeat of Nazism, the inner apotheosis of a man who wanted to free his fellow men from their shackles.

The change was triggered in 1939 by a concrete reminder of the theme of the bird flying over the plain, which was doubtless the "satori" (revelation in Zen) for which Miró had been waiting. Four pictures (measuring appromimately a meter by eighty centimeters) were executed after notations Miró made while watching the Normandy landscape go by the window of his compartment in a train. The birds he saw were crows. Not always flying in the direction the train was moving, they followed independent, sovereign, and majestic paths in a timeless space. It is not necessary to bring in Einstein and the theory of relativity to understand that as Miró jotted down his little notes on scraps of paper that day, somewhere between two train stations, while the people around him talked about whether there would be a war or not, he felt something new—a "shock" that awoke him and brought a new awareness of self. Through the intermediary of the birds' flight, he saw himself flying over the space of his life and adopted country, which he would be forced to leave in May 1940. He did not know this yet, but he may have dreaded the possibility in secret. As the

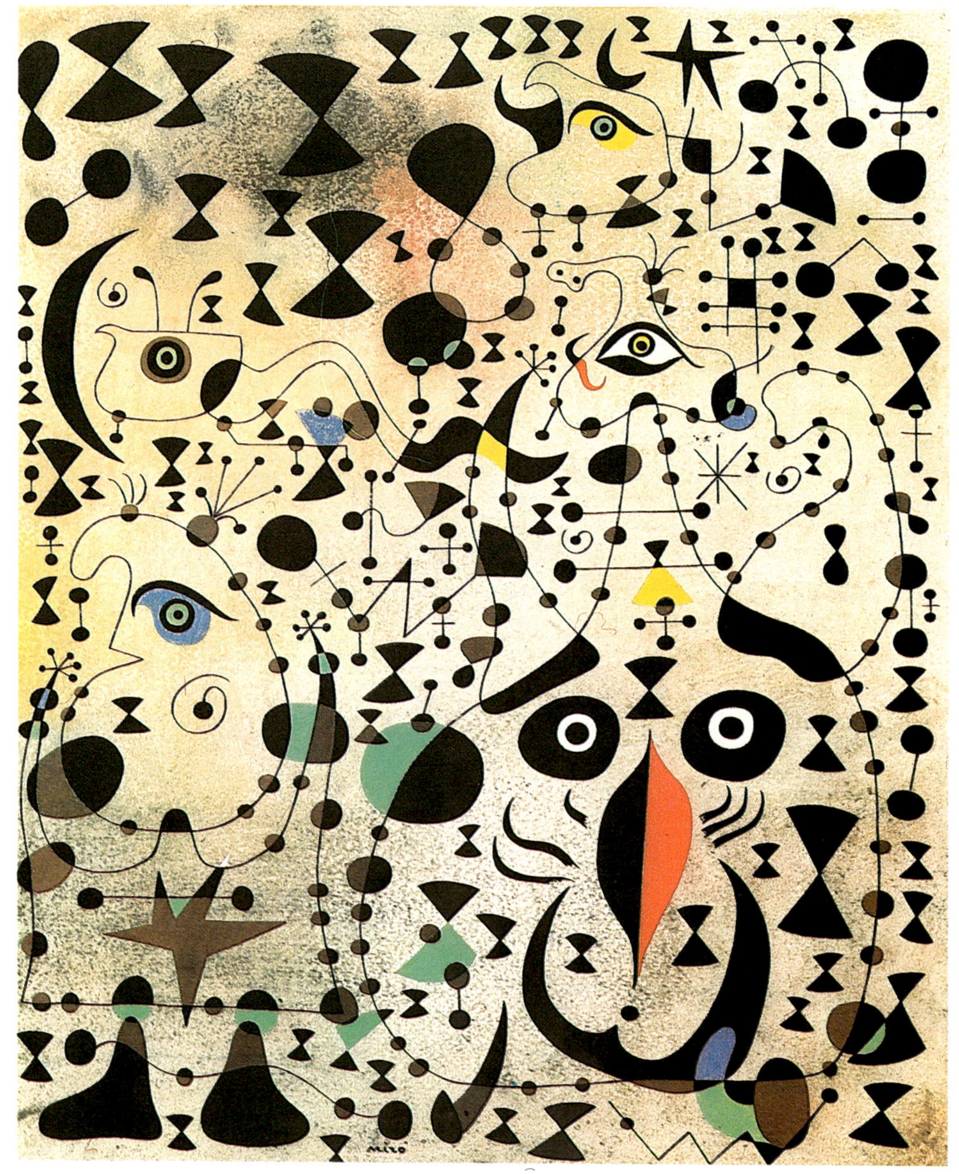

The Beautiful Bird Revealing the Unknown to a Couple in Love
1941

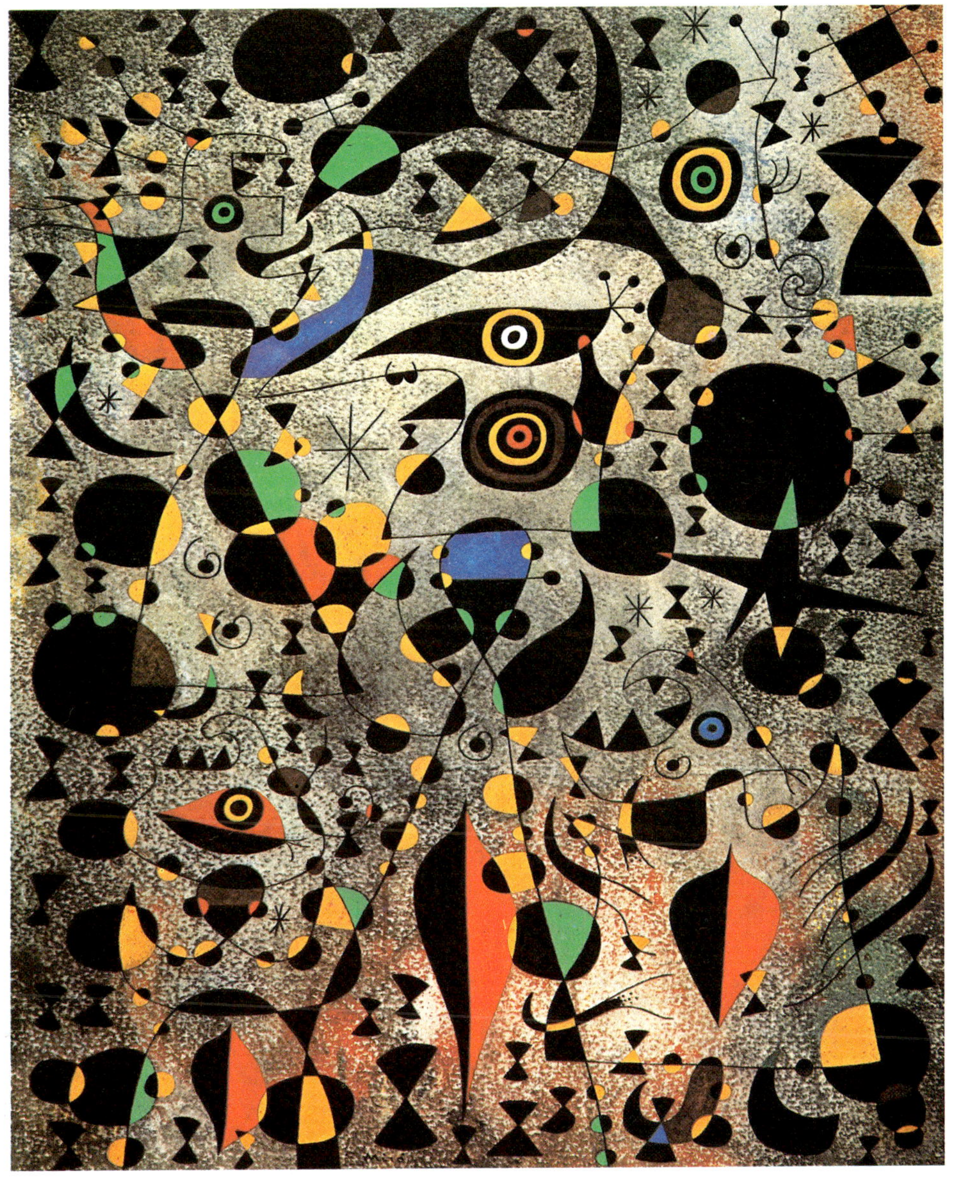

Woman Encircled
by the Flight of a Bird
1940

train advanced towards Varengeville—where Braque lived, where Breton wrote *Nadja* and Aragon his *Traité du style*—Miró knew he would have to go back to Paris and paint these four pictures; but it would be only an interlude before, back in Varengeville, he finally flung himself into the meticulous and delicate exploration of the "Constellations." Miró saw the crows flying over Normandy as signs speaking in his voice: "Whatever happens, I will follow my trajectory. No person or thing—not even war, which makes everything deviate—will cause me to lose my way. I am alone and mad, but only madness rings true. It links us to the cosmos."

Miró did not like to talk about his native country and dismissed the questions Duthuit asked him about it. He was profoundly opposed to Fascism; but Picasso, *Guernica*, and all the loud anti-Fascist declarations did not correspond to the unlimited response he was trying to formulate to it. He had made the most sincere of efforts to speak the language of the artists around him; in 1937, he had even returned to the Grande Chaumière studio where, surrounded by students and young painters, he drew nudes whose deformations and twists prove that he could have taken that route if he had really wanted to. But suddenly refusing to yield to the temptation to regress, he set out for that Mecca of Surrealism called Varengeville (where Victor Brauner would later settle too) and turned his back on the Grande Chaumière, realism, and the rhetoric of the war. He took advantage of his isolation to radicalize his formal vocabulary by lightening it and freeing it of the thickness and volume that still weighed it down. Listening to music and contemplating the stars helped him to merge into the immensity.

To do so, he had to free himself from his obsession with his native land. Narrow conceptions of "national" interest could only hinder him. "To become fully human," Miró observed, "a person must free himself from his false self. In my case, I had to stop being Miró, i.e., a Spanish painter belonging to a society limited by national boundaries and social and bureaucratic conventions. In other words, one must move towards anonymity." Miró's paradox—to individualize himself so deeply as to become anonymous—is that of all painters and poets who aim at

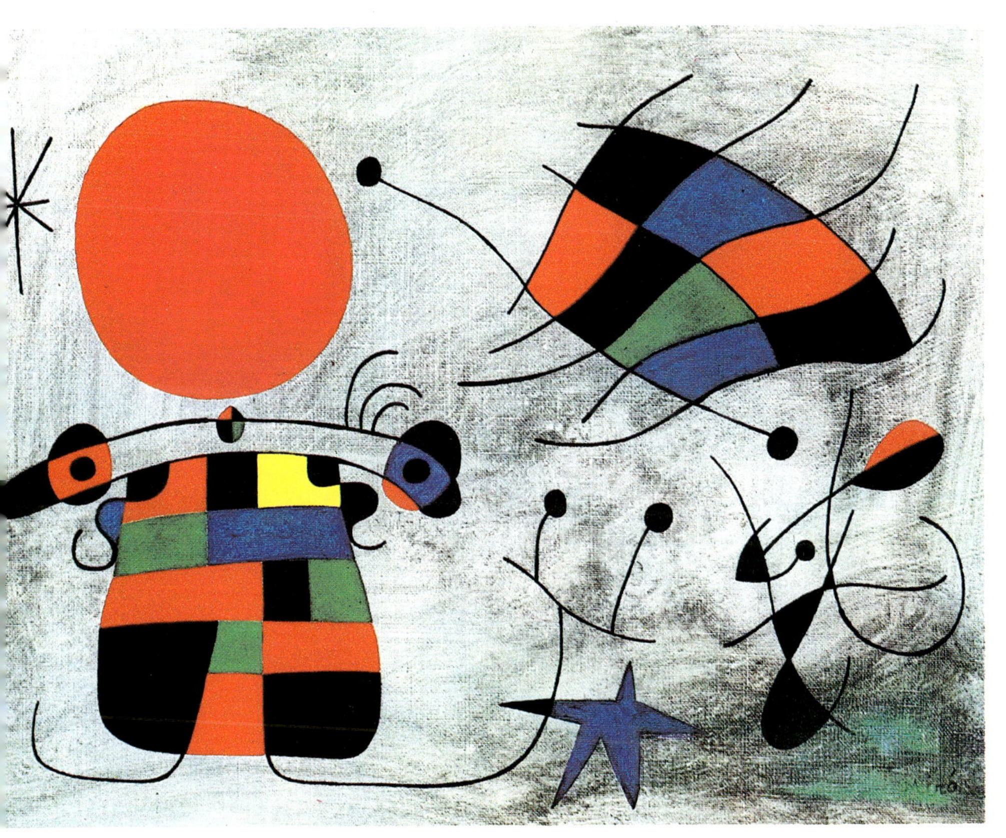

The Smile
with Blazing Wings
1953

universality. He chose this path to keep the scope of his work from being reduced to a record of contemporary events, to move toward immediacy and disclosure: the flutter of a bird's wing in the sky, a dewdrop, the twinkle of a star! Each chord is played in the void, but each and every note can be heard.

The first book on Miró was published in Tokyo in 1940. Takiguchi Shûzô, the poet who, by himself, embodies Surrealism in Japan, wrote it with love. It is not an accident if, at this bend in the road, such a surprising nod of complicity came to Miró from the other side of the globe, placing him where he belonged: between two civilizations, two flutters of history. In 1941, the first retrospective of his work, organized by J. J. Sweeney, opened at the Museum of Modern Art in New York, thus consecrating Miró in the gateway to America where, through the impetus of the Surrealists who took refuge there the following year, painting would soon begin emitting new signs. Neither Japan nor the United States had a modern language of its own; and the fact that Miró was one of the very first to nourish the hope of finding one was certainly no accident. Sensitive to Far Eastern calligraphy, his drawing never imitated it, but was not foreign to it. What fascinated Miró about calligraphy was not so much the actual graphics as the fact that ideographic communication transcends spoken language and, thanks to the Chinese characters, the particularity of languages. He wanted for painting to crystallize a new shared sense of things.

By opting for a universal language of silent signs, Miró was able to avoid the trap the Mexican painters fell into: that of promoting national identity, which condemns those who get caught in it to define themselves only negatively in relation to others. "All this talk about the nation is just a lot of bureaucracy!" Miró said. "I want to be a human being, not a bureaucrat!" Due to the simplicity of his vocabulary and his powers of poetic evocation, Miró was able to create mural paintings that are not propaganda posters. The Surrealists never identified—not even on the walls of official buildings—with any country, least of all their own: Miró no more than Max Ernst or Matta. Is this to say that Miró stopped being Miró? His true self was mobile. He tore his Harlequin's coat to shreads: each piece was only a tiny part of an individual who brought about his own explosion and expansion to infinity. By finding signs of self everywhere (in the stones he picked up and the objects he stumbled on, which he later turned into sculptures), Miró finally merged with the world of chance. No longer anyone, he became "anonymous." Miró did not go toward things, birds, and stars. The resonating things of the cosmos came to him...

Had he become the bird caught in the giant, ghostly hand in his 1926 picture, the bird that seems to be sucking the finger in *Hand Catching a Bird*? Had bird-hand-Miró become one to create, cry out, write, scribble, paint, and shine? Was it not that bird which drew the "Constellations"? Was it not that bird which conceived the "escape ladder" of January 31, 1940, ten days after *Sunrise*, in which the flying bird was still the crow seen from the compartment window of the train chugging across Normandy? Up to May 14, 1940, Miró continued, in Varengeville, the series of gouaches where for the first time everything dances, intersects and criss-crosses in a single harmonious cosmogony. When he resumed this series in Palma de Mallorca in September, with *The Nightingale's Song at Midnight and the Morning Rain*, the very same cosmic music would seem to have followed him from France to Spain, with no break in tone whatsoever. In the second gouache done in Palma, *On the 13th the Ladder Brushed the Firmament*, which dates from October 14, all the planets and all the stars—or nearly so—are interconnected, as if the whole sky had become the text of a single poem.

Oddly removed from these gouaches, the poems André Breton wrote on them from October to December 1958, seventeen years after the series had been finished, do not express the planetary music that contemplating the "Constellations" produces in us. Autonomous and sovereign in relation to the gouaches, Breton's poems seem to be intentionally speaking of something entirely different—of Lamiel, for example, brandishing a torch and getting ready to burn down the Law Courts (*la Poétesse*); it is as if the poet could express this star-filled universe only in terms of female figures and the feeling of voluptuousness it procured him: "Luxury," he said, "is found in voluptuousness." Breton's poems are a transposition of Miró's metaphoric vocabulary—which is not to say that Breton forgets "the little, naked man who has the key to the puzzle" (Miró himself?), "who teaches the *language of the birds*" (*l'Oiseau migrateur*)—and, at the same time, a private meditation stimulated by the painter's monument to the infinity of the universe and his own basic disequilibrium, to everything *uneven* about himself.

The series of "Constellations" is made up of twenty-three gouaches—not twenty-two, the figure given by Breton, who neglected to write a poem on *Nocturne*. Miró, who hated even numbers, intentionally chose this figure: "to wreck the smugness of those who say 2 plus 2 is 4," he wrote in *De l'assassinat de la peinture à la céramique*. "What we need is for 2 plus 2 to equal 13." In Miró, order is never symmetrical; and the "Constellations" correspond neither to the twelve tones of the dodecaphonic series nor to the twenty-two cards of the major arcana in tarot. In Miró, there is always a foot or a hand too many.

Once he had finished this uninterrupted series of masterpieces, Miró settled in Barcelona in 1942, in the apartment where he was born, and lived there with his mother until 1944. His mother died, and his liberation was complete. Nothing weighed on him any longer. He identified with the air and space—mentally occupying it from within and without— with his birds, his women, and his stars, and relied on color and drawing alone to make them exist. They seem to have painted themselves, as if the painting machine, perfectly oiled, were running all by itself.

Jacques Dupin attributed this grace to the fact that Miró had stopped using exterior models and, moreover, "bringing the unconscious into play." Can we really be sure of this? Living in the apartment of his birth with his mother, was not Miró closer than ever to the unconscious? Dupin's interpretation—which has something of a condemnation about it—exemplifies the kind of attitude that has made it possible for some to hint that Miró was not really a Surrealist at all. He "sunk inwards," Dupin writes:

but where, if not into those dynamic—unconscious or semi-conscious—spaces that resist aesthetic analysis? Is this just more bickering over semantics? Perhaps "unconscious" is not the right word. In any case, it seems clear that Miró, from the "Constellations" on, created out of the accidents of matter and the irregularities of paper in a way that called something very like the unconscious into play. Miró's vocabulary was not lightened or freed by any orders he gave himself, and even less by a grammar or syntax—as in Mondrian's case; it was born and proliferated simultaneously with the act of its own creation. It ordered itself spontaneously, with the automatic naturalness of a morning glory. Miró's *Catalan Notebooks* make it perfectly clear that preliminary sketches for his paintings were no longer indispensable after 1941. The automatism that guided his notes, which were usually very rough indications used to position the figures, was called back into play when Miró took up his brush, and he painted quite freely in relation to them. Between 1942 and 1945, Miró invented his definitive "writing," plunging into solitude and Bach, or Mozart, or going to listen to the organist practicing in the Barcelona cathedral, where he was wont to contemplate the light filtering through the stained-glass windows. His experience of music and light allowed him to draw his images more directly, in a lighter and more musical hand than ever. It got him to wander mentally on the paper, for he had not yet dared to go all the way and tackle the canvas without preliminaries, as he began doing in 1945-1946. Jacques Dupin expresses this better than anyone: "His figures ignore each other; they multiply without seeing each other, their lines intersecting without them touching; their neighbors establish no relationship whatsoever with them. They are strangers to each other and absolutely alone. They do, however, have one thing in common which gives unity to the work and its characteristic strong, wild identity to everything Miró does: the extremely intense space that bathes them, or rather out of which they emerge. This phenomenon has no equivalent if not, perhaps, the superimposition and entanglement of animal representations in paleolithic wall art which prehistorians sometimes call 'sketchbooks.' "

Abandoning "scenes," Harlequins, angry Catalan peasants, hunters and

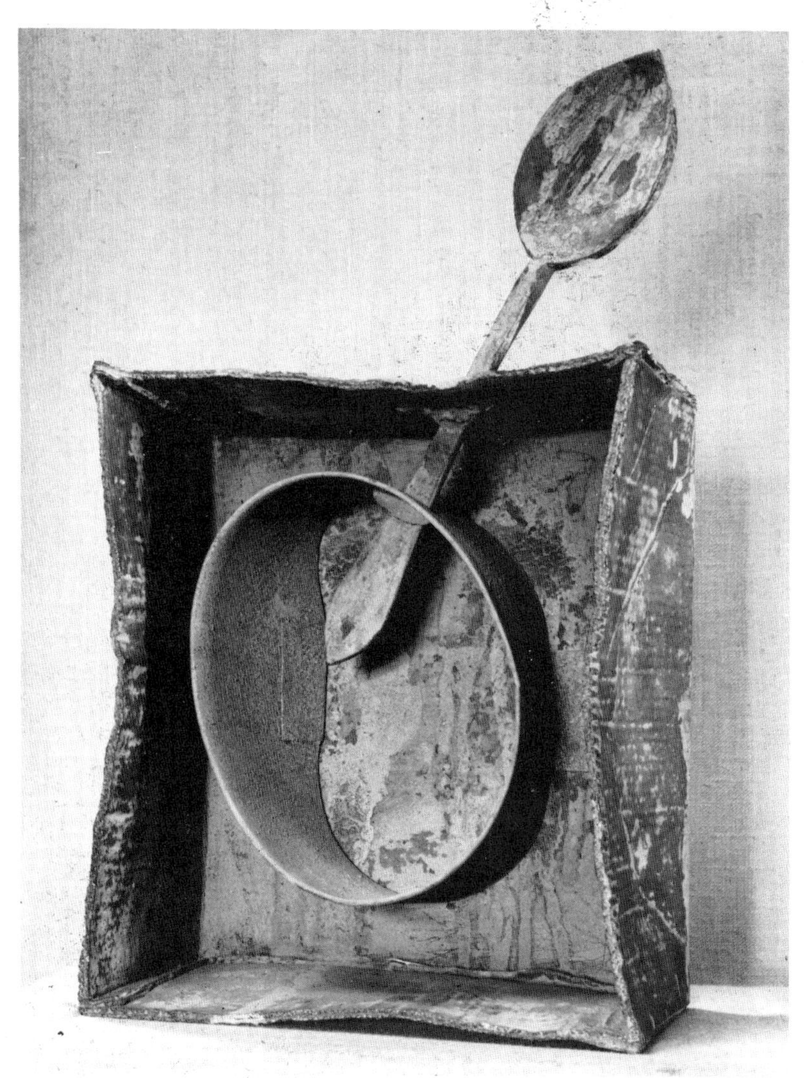

The Wind-Clock
1967

reapers, Miró began painting his signs on a sort of immense "makimono," the only fictional supports of which are the sky and water. At age fifty-two, Miró stopped listening to everyone, because he thought he could hear his own song in the galaxy. Where was it emanating from? From what inner world? The unconscious is not a form of transcendence; and yet Joan Miró read John of the Cross and Teresa of Avila. For Miró, the unconscious, as he mysteriously suggested to Yvon Taillandier, was "a motionless motion," "the equivalent of what is called the eloquence of silence or what Saint John of the Cross described as a silent music." A little-known, completely vertical work (226x18 cm.), *Women, Birds, Droplets, Stars* (1944) lists, like an illustrated alphabet primer, the elements of this enchanted series, which was later to be amplified and dramatized, then to reverberate on large surfaces for an immense ideal public.

When Breton spoke of Miró's "Constellations" again as a new kind of beauty linking the existence of the figures to music and silence, he mentioned neither the unconscious nor automatism, as if he had forgotten the words; and instead of evoking the war during which they were created, he preferred to speak of "transcendence" and the "eternalness" of beauty. But was he not actually confronted with the blooming of a totally new and fragile beauty constantly renewing itself?

According to Deleuze and Guattari, "becoming a bird" can happen only "to the extent that the bird is itself in the process of becoming something else, pure line and pure color"—which is exactly the case for Miró, whom they neglect to mention. Their main reference is Klee. It is true that, in his very last works in 1940, Klee was moving towards a graphic expression as simple and direct as Miró's—in *Death and Fire* and *Timpanist*, for example—although he abandoned it in his *Final Still Life*. Unbeknownst to Klee, Miró was overtaking him on his own road, for Klee remained a prisoner of conscious themes and symbols ("death," "fire") and traditional subjects ("still life") to the end. By definitively freeing himself from these during the war, Miró freed painting from its ideological heritage. So doing, he also linked it to art's pre-artistic origins in paleolithic wall frescoes, prior to all the "ideologies," "theories," and even "aesthetics" of picture-making. The painter cast his die into the sky, which was beautiful long before men started making art. The beauty of Miró's painting lies in a return to the innocence of the sky and its implacable, anonymous beauty.

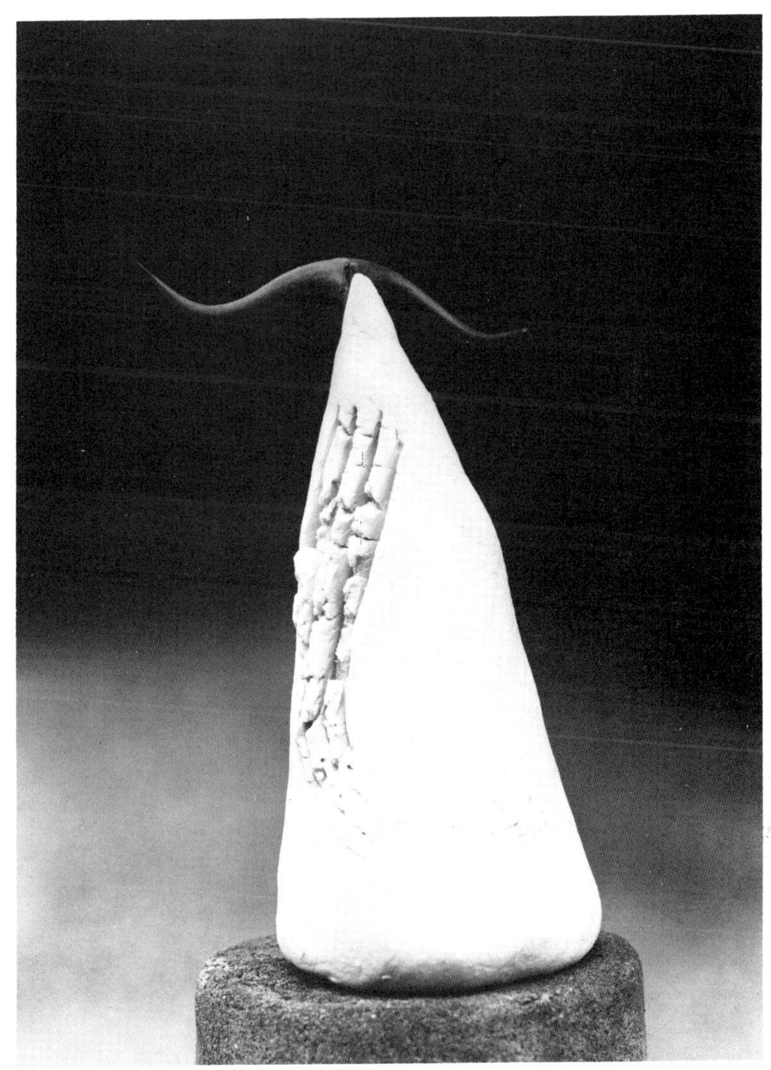

Porcelain
1981

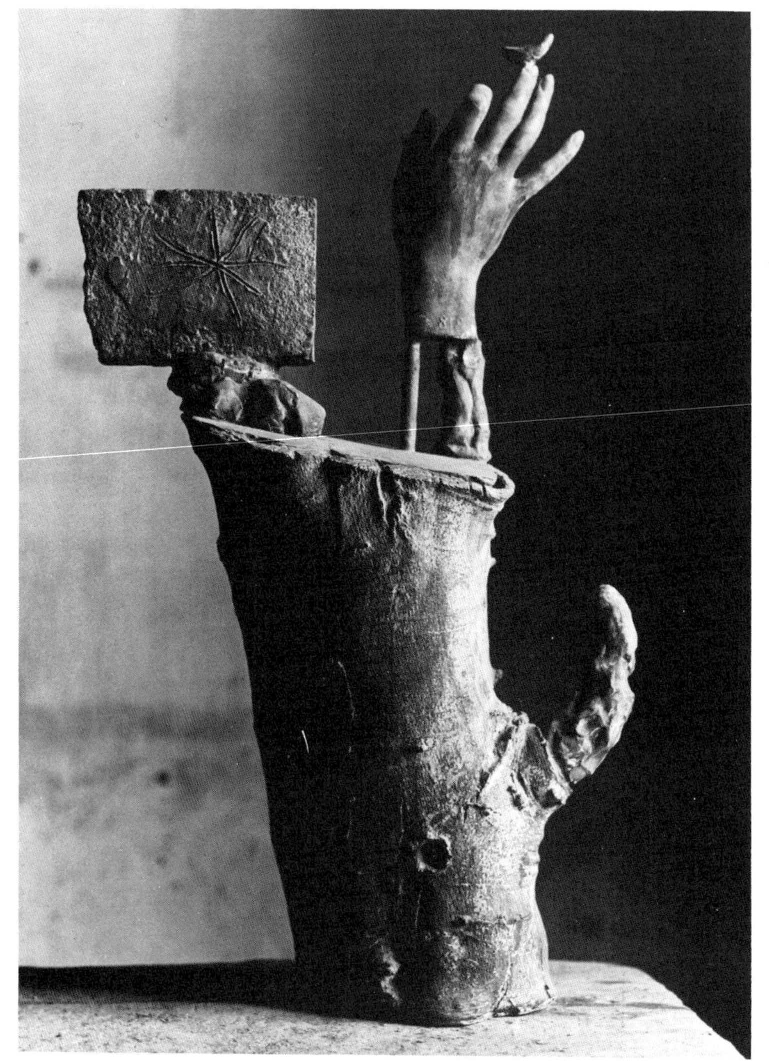

Bird Nesting in Fingers in Bloom
1969

THE FUSION OF THE SPIRIT OF DADA AND THE GESTURES OF PREHISTORY

I first saw paintings of Miró's in 1945-1946 when I chanced to go into the gallery of (I later learned) Simone Collinet, André Breton's first wife.

They were displayed alongside three or four paintings by Yves Tanguy, one of which had been shot up by German officers during the Occupation. I have often evoked my shock at seeing this "executed" picture.* And my shock hampered my discovery of Miró. At the time, I knew next to nothing about either painter; but it was not only because of the vandalism that Tanguy's paintings fascinated me first. They opened onto a new three-dimensional space where I thought I recognized the landscapes of a new planet at dawn. And what was missing in Miró's freer, less representational way of thinking was this illusion of a real space inviting the imagination in. Tanguy's paintings gave me the feeling I was traveling in a dream; but where could my thoughts wander in Miró's signs? Were they to be read like writing, from top to bottom, or bottom to top? Was one to slide over their surface the way one climbs up a wall to jump down into the street? In Tanguy (and this idea grew even stronger the day I entered Breton's studio for the first time in late 1946), I felt as if I were on the deck of a ship pitching in the sea (and I have never been able to think of Tanguy's name without thinking of *tanguer*, which in French means "to pitch and roll"), while in Miró—whom I did not dare think about—I found myself nowhere.

Nowhere? Could it be that the freest painting takes place nowhere? Or in another, fourth, or fifth dimension? Did this mean that Miró was no longer painting by projecting images from his mind? What was he doing? Was he making his figures rise out of the canvas itself? Was he approaching submerged objects so closely that they became flat? But how and why were they, in spite of everything, rendered in such a visible, clear and concrete way? What was the sleight-of-hand? It was fleeting questions like these that

* For example, in *Le Monde est un tableau* (Paris, Pierre Bordas et fils, 1979).

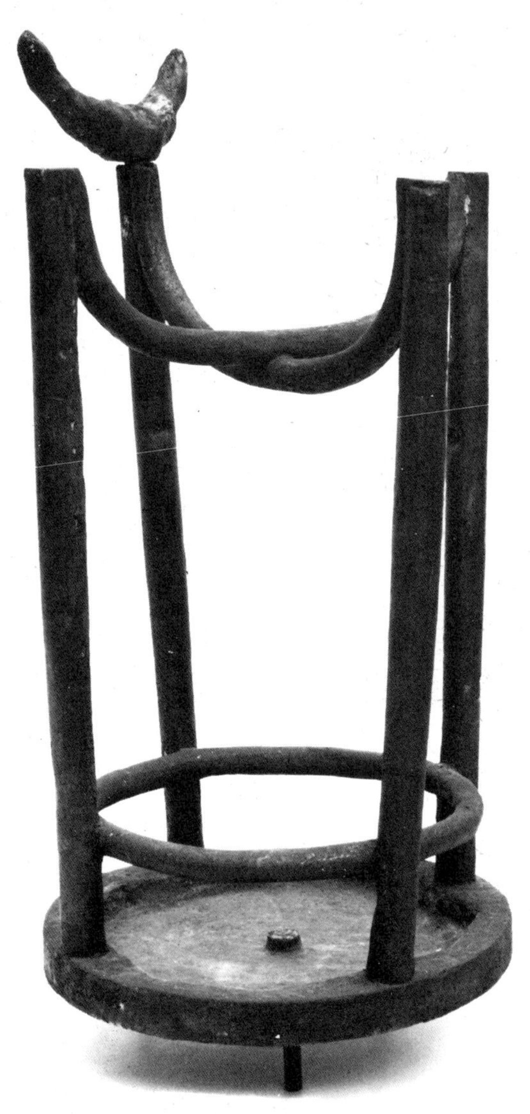

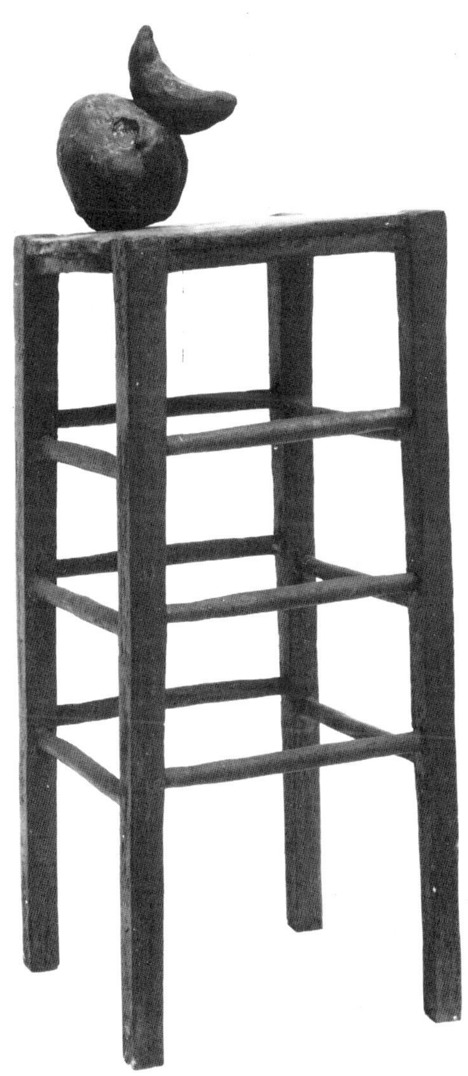

Man and Woman in the Night
1969

I must have been asking myself, stunned as I was by the forms of an art that had been hidden from my generation for the entire duration of the Occupation.

A year later, in 1947, Miró spent eight months in the United States, from February to October; greater and stronger than before, he reemerged from the silence and isolation in which he had shut himself during the war. If the United States was a shock for him, it was that of a giant opening: a beautiful overture. The success that greeted his work allowed him to pass to a higher plane—from a minor to a major key, from an individual to a collective register—without losing the secrets of his little night music. But the great shift in values that was then beginning—emphasizing the contestation of Surrealism and increasing the prestige of lesser pre-war avant-gardes—did not catch Miró unprepared. Instead of resisting this shift, Miró committed himself to it totally. The door opened to him in the United States was but a pretext for him to go beyond everything he had accomplished previously and carry his investigations to the limit in all of the media he explored: ceramics (with his friend Artigas), sculpture (which took on enormous importance in his work from 1966 on), engraving, and lithography. It is as if the repressed power channeled into the intimate world of his earlier works had been condemned by events to explode late. His return in 1948 to Paris, where the Galerie Maeght was beginning to display his works and where, the previous year, he had participated in the international Surrealist exhibition, marked the beginning of a new expansion that brought him worldwide recognition as the greatest postwar painter—the painter of exploding subjectivity.

In 1949-1950, Miró accomplished the feat of painting, in just a few months' time, two contrasting series of pictures: the "slow paintings" and the "spontaneous paintings." Based on two speeds that produce two different languages out of the same basic vocabulary, this was an utterly astounding period. The "slow paintings" are untitled, as are the "spontaneous" ones (apart from a few exceptions). In the two series, Miró emitted the same signs, but compared what happened when he drew them with precision and

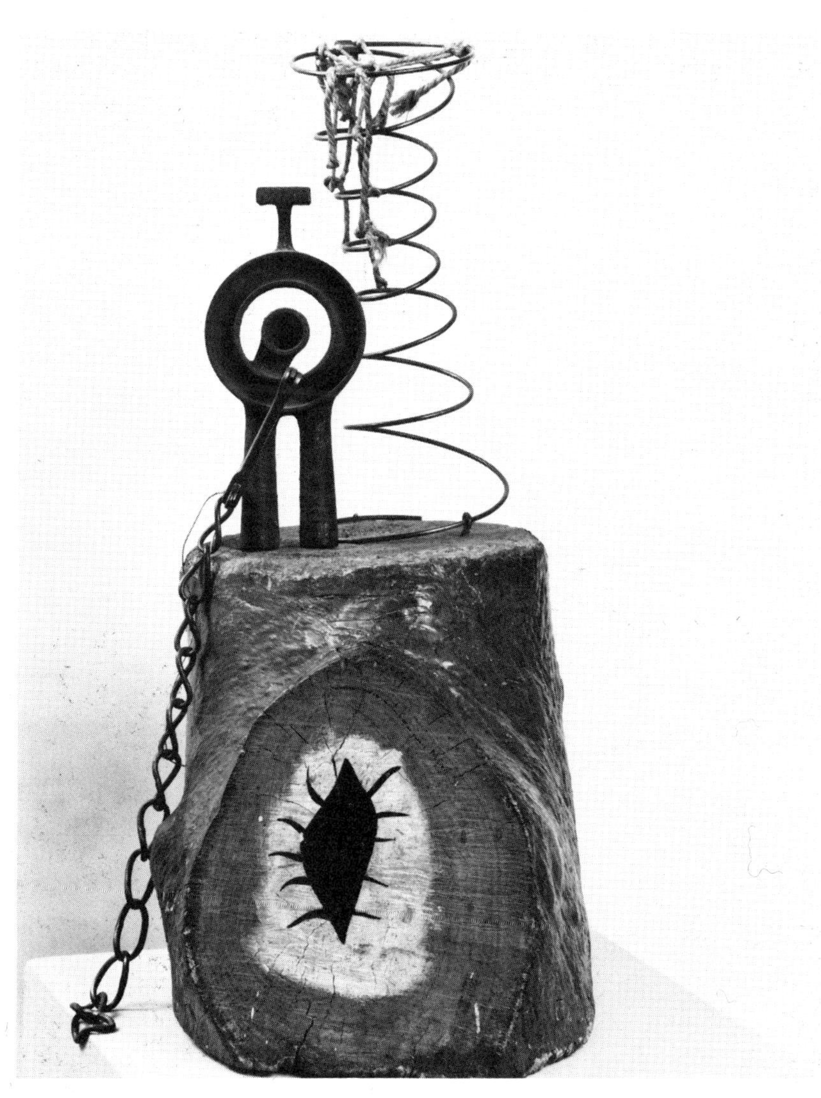

Object of Sunset
1937

what happened when he painted them applying long strokes with the ardor and intense concentration of energy of Zen monks doing large-format calligraphy. Working on a more carefully prepared ground each time, he never repeated himself. Each series, and each painting, is distinct.

In 1919, when they wrote *les Champs magnétiques* (the working title of which was *les Précipités*), Breton and Soupault had attempted to write at varying speeds; but their experiment involved only varying degrees of acceleration. In chapters like "Saisons," memory (Breton's childhood memories) attached itself to the movement of the slowest sentences. The faster the two poets went, the less time memory had to rush into the dizzying blanks between the words and commas. Similarly, Miró's signs interconnect and combine together elegantly in the "slow paintings," and are brutally isolated from each other in the "spontaneous" ones. Does the unconscious emerge more clearly in the latter? No, but it does emerge in a different way. As it stakes out its territory, its glides, figures, curls, and junctions are more fleeting. In preparing the grounds for these canvases, Miró changed the givens of his own "automatic writing." It is as if Breton and Soupault had written their poem on sheets partially covered with barely visible sentences that, here and there, their writing met up with in passing.

When Miró realized this double series, I was just beginning to write about painting. I followed his work from afar, silently, the way one follows sailboats gliding over the sea. I was still learning to judge the direction of the winds. "Abstract expressionism" and "tachisme" appeared on the scene; paintings took shape quickly, rather than in the heavy slowness of geometric abstraction. In his own particular way, Miró short-circuited both ways of seeing and showing; but nobody understood this—excepting Jacques Dupin, who was quick to understand what had happened. But, in the world of art, things were already turning sour. Fashion, which had always been foreign to painting, was in the process of infiltrating it; and, encouraged by dealers and critics, painters were yielding more and more often to the contradictory temptation to be guided by systems that had nothing to do with themselves. Well before 1968, the development of the

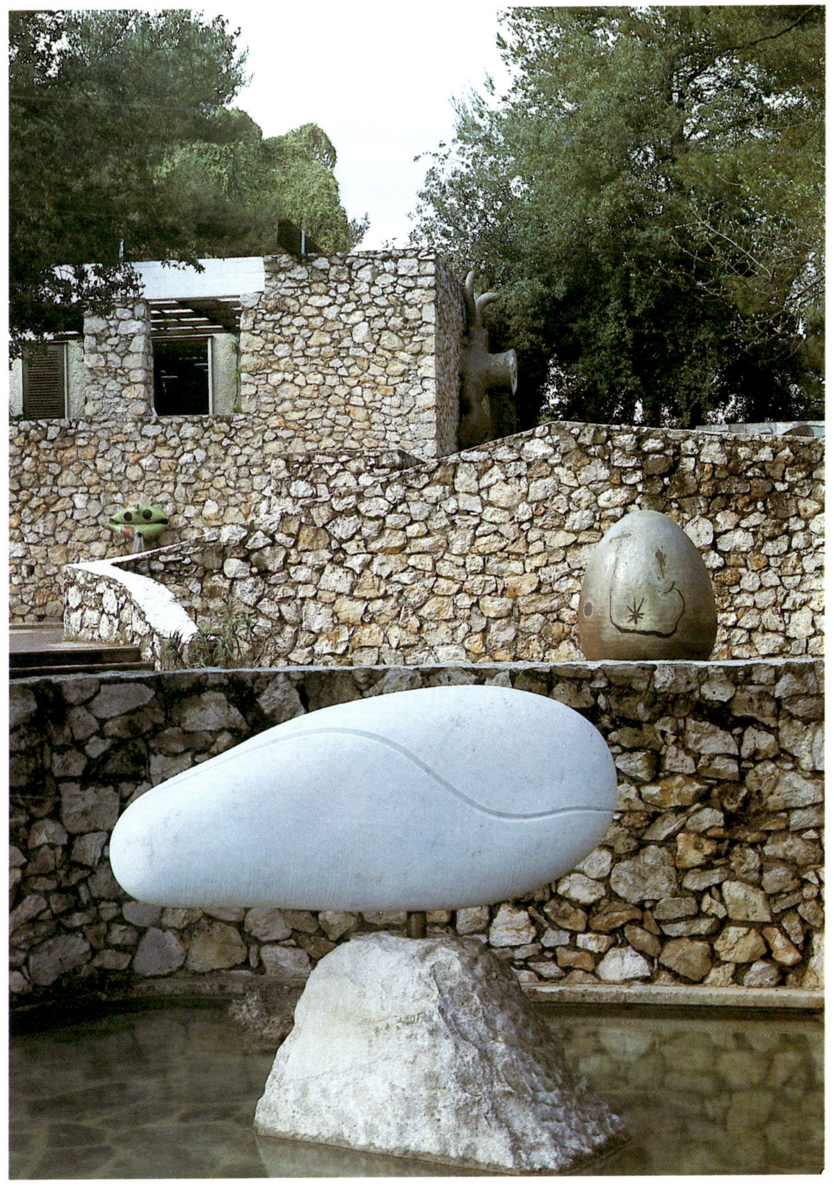

Woman with Dishevelled Hair
1968

media was contributing to this; and it took a certain courage to resist and not "change colors" every five or ten years.

Margit Rowell reminds us that Miró went to Jackson Pollock's first one-man exhibition in Paris in March, 1952; and it was, as Miró himself told Georges Duthuit, a "revelation." Besides the fact that it was Surrealists exiled in New York during the war who had "revealed" the techniques of automatism to the American painters, it should not be forgotten that Miró had not waited for this "revelation" to give free reign to stains and splashes of color, as can be seen, for example, in the 1950 *Painting* reproduced in Dupin's book. Miró had begun using larger formats in 1945-1946; later, his "desire to expand" was strengthened by the American painters' generalized use of giant formats, which had been used only by Picasso and Léger before them. However, the fact that Miró had gone to the United States in 1947, met Pollock in Hayter's studio (where American painters were learning to apply the techniques of automatism to engraving) and shown an interest in Pollock's investigations in no way authorizes one to say that these painters were moving in a direction he had wanted to take, but had not dared to follow up to then or that "this freedom of gesture encouraged him to turn toward a more spontaneous kind of pictorial expression." Since 1924, all of his energies had been concentrated in this direction! He was the real pioneer!

Miró's pictures are pictures in the sense that Novalis gave the word: "A picture is not an allegory or the symbol of something else; it is the symbol of itself." In the 20th century, Surrealism has been the greatest source of such pictures; and Miró's are the most sovereign of them all. The (concrete) Surrealization of the unknown images and forms of the unconscious—their discovery, exploration, and investigation—was the defining characteristic of Surrealist activity, in painting as in poetry. Liking to tread on the soil because, as he so beautifully said, "strength enters through the feet," Miró invented a Surrealism of the soil, which allowed the spontaneous associations of his unconscious to branch out and upward into the stars, sometimes into the void. Long realized in a minor key, his project was to rediagram man's relations with nature in order to shake up the old scientific and religious conceptions of man and the order of nature. To do so, he relied on irregularity, unevenness, contradiction, disequilibrium, and humor. The organic elaboration of his work cannot be separated from the chance that governs our random, exploding, unfinished universe; yet he had to endow his sculptures with a provocativeness that rivals Duchamp's for it to be remembered that his inner movement cannot be dissociated from the fundamental Surrealist desire to shake things up—and in this, he remained utterly loyal to the spirit of Dada.

In his early "objects"—e.g., *Man and Woman* (1931), *Poetic Object* (1936), *Object of Sunset* (1938)—Miró transformed things into signs. He instinctively chose these objects in function of his formal vocabulary; and, consequently, they cannot be dissociated from his painting, especially since he quite often applied painted signs to them and, in 1932, even entitled one of them *Painting-Object*. All of these objects illustrate what Breton called "dignifying the found object." But Miró, rarely isolating the objects he found in the paths of Palma, associated and combined them, thus anticipating Robert Rauschenberg's "combine-paintings" by nearly thirty years. At the same time, he rejected Duchamp's ready-mades—in spite of his great admiration for that artist—and *aided*, more or less, his own ready-mades.* For a long time, he did not suspect their ephemeral character; many of them have deteriorated, or been lost. After the war, he had the objects he found cast in bronze. One of the most famous of these is the 1963 *Pitchfork* with five prongs that he defiantly installed on the terrace of his "labyrinth" at the Fondation Maeght. Miró usually identified these objects with animate figures—women, birds, a "crowned head," a "woman-dog"—and entitled two stools—one upright, the other upside down—*Man and Woman in the Night* (1969). These substitutions create a magical kind of hallucinatory presence and recall the game of "One in the Other," invented by the Surrealists after the war, which involved identifying oneself with an object or thing and describing it as a different

* *Miró sculptures*, by Alain Jouffroy and Teixidor, Maeght éditeur, 1974.

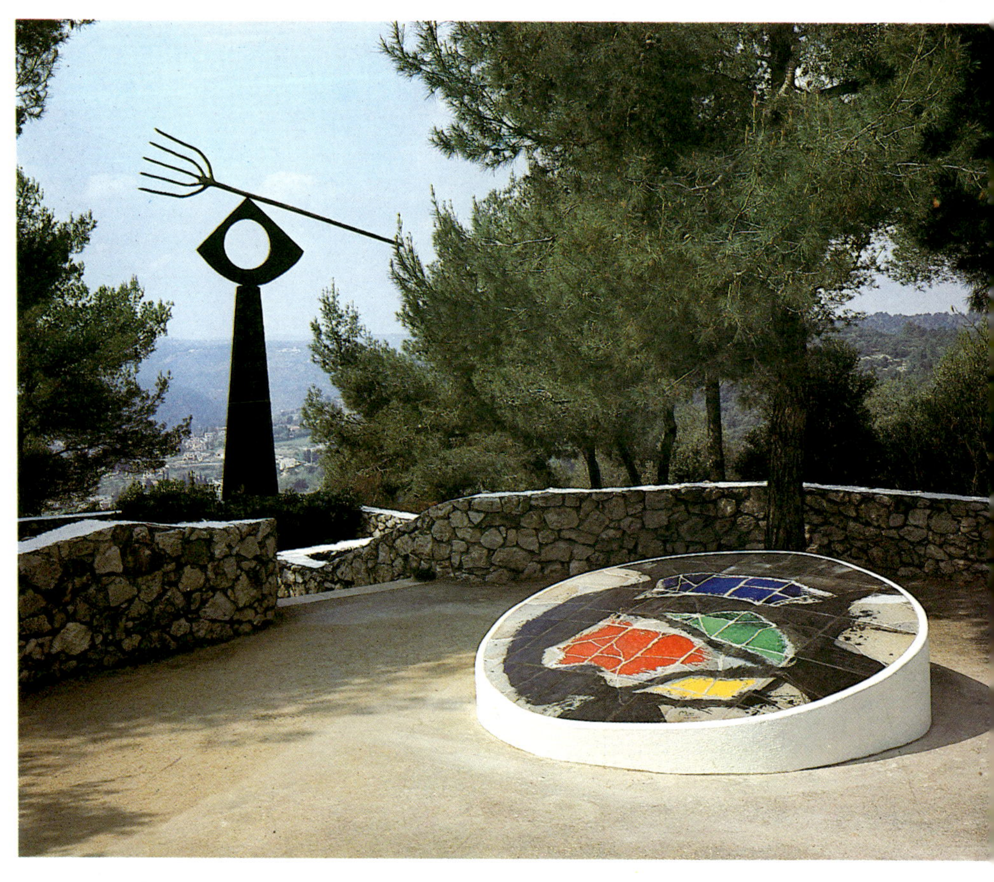

Pitchfork
1963

object or thing chosen by your partners. Consider an example from Toyen:

> I am a big, flat HAT on the ground, made of criss-crossing ribbons that stretch out and disappear on the horizon,

an indirect way of saying—through substitution—that she was identifying with a crossroads. In Miró, the stools substitute for the man and woman just as in Toyen a hat substitutes for the intersection. Is it an accident if, without realizing it, Miró here, as elsewhere, coincided with the secret evolution of the movement in which he had participated in his youth? Certainly not, for everything he painted, sculpted, modeled, engraved, and lithographed from 1950 to his death is stamped with the Surrealist poetics of automatism and the found object. To begin his first text on "Surrealism and Painting," Breton wrote in 1928:

> The eye exists in an untamed state. The only witness of the Wonders of the Earth at an altitude of thirty meters and the Wonders of the Sea at a depth of thirty meters is the wild eye that can see colors only in terms of the rainbow. It presides over the conventional exchange of signals that the mind's navigations would seem to require. But who will set up the ladder of vision?

In a most uncanny way, every single one of these words holds for Miró and, indeed, applies to him more than to any other Surrealist painter: the wildness of the eye, the Wonders of the Earth and Sea, the rainbow, signals, mind's navigations, and ladder of vision. Everything happened as if Miró had not needed to read or hear these words to dedicate himself entirely, throughout his life, to what they evoke and signify. When he wrote them, Breton may have been thinking of the beautiful "Landscapes" Miró had just invented in 1926 and 1927: *Horse at the Seaside*, the landscapes known as *On the Banks of the River of Love* and *The Hare*, *Landscape with Rooster*, *Animated Landscape*—all of which are large paintings—and *Dog Barking at the Moon*, in which a ladder rises into the void of the sky. He may also have been thinking of Tanguy's 1927 evocations of the ocean depths, e.g., *Turning Out the Lights We Don't Need*; *Mom, Dad Has Been Wounded*; and *A Big Picture Representing a Landscape*, in which Breton had just recognized the reinvented image of Ys, the submerged city. Between

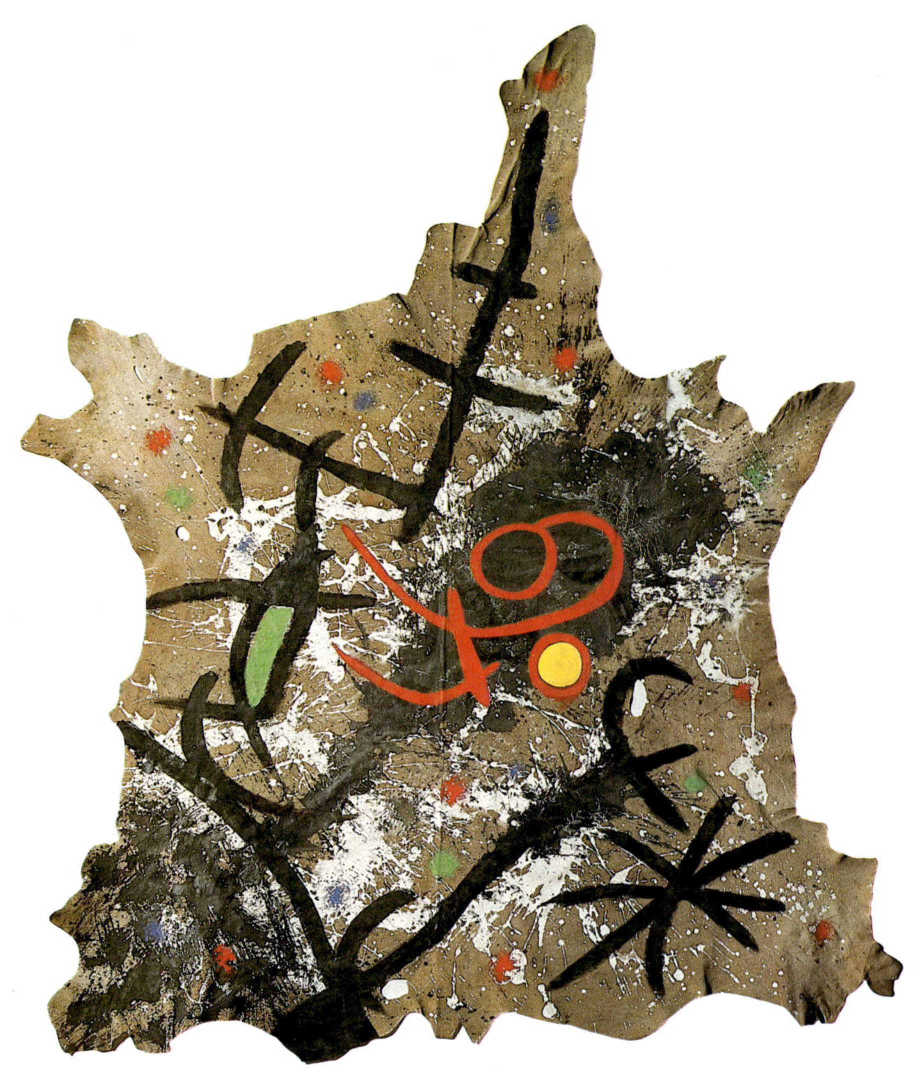

Birds of Prey
Swooping Down on Our Shadows
1970

Tanguy and Miró, Breton was still in search of the "mental world at the stage of Genesis"; but it seems likely that, thanks to these two painters, he had already had a "*non-legendary* glimpse" of this world and could thus launch the universal drift that led painting out of its old territories.

"I am neither an engraver nor a painter, but rather someone who tends to express himself however he can," Miró once said. Trivial though it may seem, this little remark says everything about Miró. *Someone* (not an artist, not a painter, not an engraver) *who tends to express himself however he can* leaves out the greatest, and most illusory, reference of all: art itself! Like prehistoric man painting on the smoothest parts of rock walls with bones, his fingers, wadded plants, clumps of hair, chewed-up sticks and, at Lascaux, hollow tubes (through which magnesium and iron oxide powder were blown), Miró used anything and everything to realize his engravings: little knives, toothpicks, toothbrushes, goose feathers. He sometimes even put his copperplates in a henhouse so that they would be clawed and pecked up before he actually began engraving. Mentioning a number of examples, Blandine Bouret comments that "Miró's spontaneity and violence call the finality of art into question. No longer a question of contemplating beauty, it becomes a brutal reminder of a forgotten truth." What truth did Miró evoke, if not that the need "to express oneself however one can" is prior to "art" itself? Art was never Miró's point of reference.

Prehistoric art is an anachronism that ignores the fact that from the Brassempouy "Head," Lespugue "Venus" and Lascaux cave paintings up to the very late birth of the notion of art, men "expressed themselves however they could" without feeling the slightest need to invent such a notion. (It is interesting to note that the word "geijutsu," the equivalent of the word "art" in Japanese—which might be translated literally as "the technique of talent"—was coined only in the late 19th century, during the Meiji era, when the Japanese imported so many Western concepts).

That did not stop the prehistorians—starting with Lastet and Choisy, who published the first study on "Quaternary Art" in 1870—from projecting the academic notion of "art" back onto the "ceiling" paintings at Altamira, discovered in 1879, at a time when such revelations still inspired fear. As Virgilio Gilardoni wrote in a book that Henri Michaux recommended to me (*The Birth of Art*): "Art was not born once and for all, on a specific day in human history. It has been rediscovered and reinvented every time a man has stepped back from practical preoccupations to question things, objects, events and appearances, and yielded to the pleasure of seeking out magical spaces in which to venture—to run, to fly, to feel—in the plenitude of human awareness. ... Art does not exist; only works of art exist." Leonardo da Vinci, who thought that "painting began as nothing but a line traced around a human shadow on the wall," was wrong: the pictures of prehistoric hunters found in Valltorta and Perrero, Spain, are not shadows, but automatic, gestural inventions, moving figures. Like Michaux, Miró knew this, and was certainly comforted by it. Prehistory helped him to free himself from the "laws of history."

Discussing the main room at Lascaux, Georges Bataille remarked that, though it was formed by "chance alone," "its proportions are so beautiful that no-one could imagine a change that would have improved them." In *Birds of Prey Swooping Down on Our Shadows*, a painting on cowhide done in 1970, the rhythm of the brutal signs Miró placed on extremely agitated white grounds was determined by the irregular outline of the hide and recalls the way the animals at Lascaux are distributed in function of the relief of the rocky walls—in the central cavity, for example, where a black bull was painted over other animal figures.

In their enigmaticness, the "unintelligible signs," grids, and blazons on the walls at Lascaux—which have been variously seen as tools, traps, and tribal signs—remind us of the checkerboard of figures hovering in some of the pictures Miró painted in 1953, such as *The Smile with Blazing Wings* and *Eyes Fixed on the Horizon Shattered by the Cries of Eagles*. The comparison also holds for the nearly empty pictures Miró painted one day in 1961, *Blue I*, *Blue II* and *Blue III*, in which several enormous black suspension points in the blue sky cannot but remind us of the series of discs

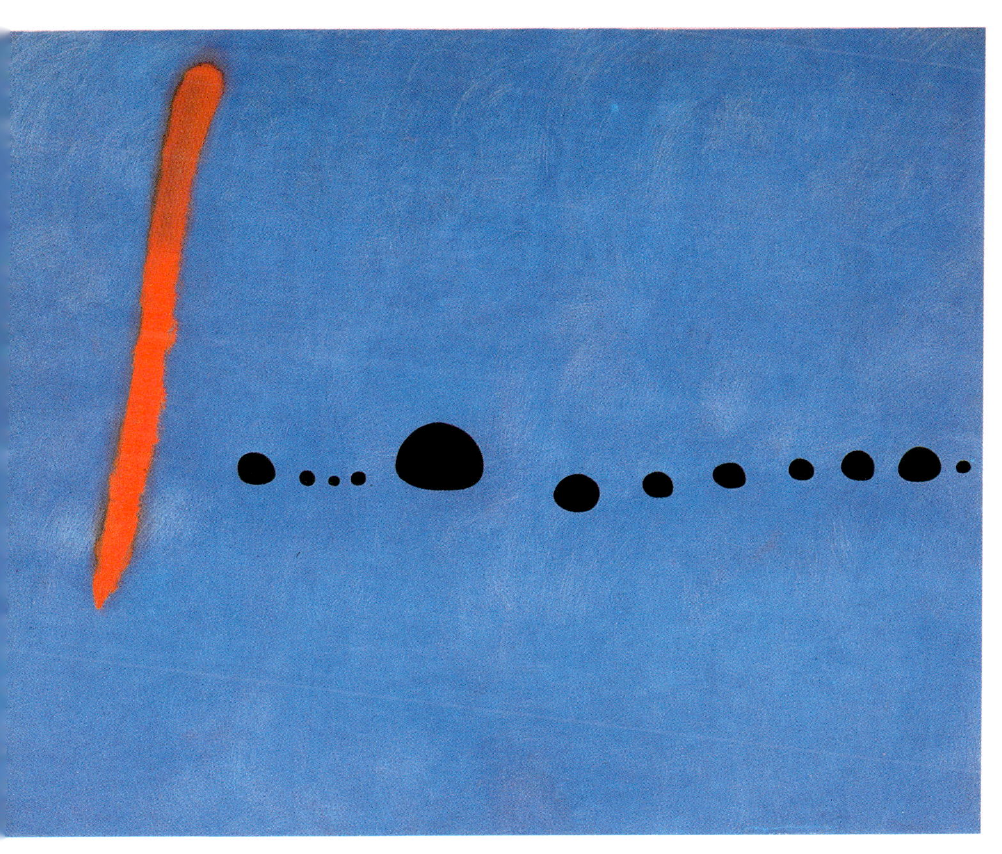

Blue II
1961

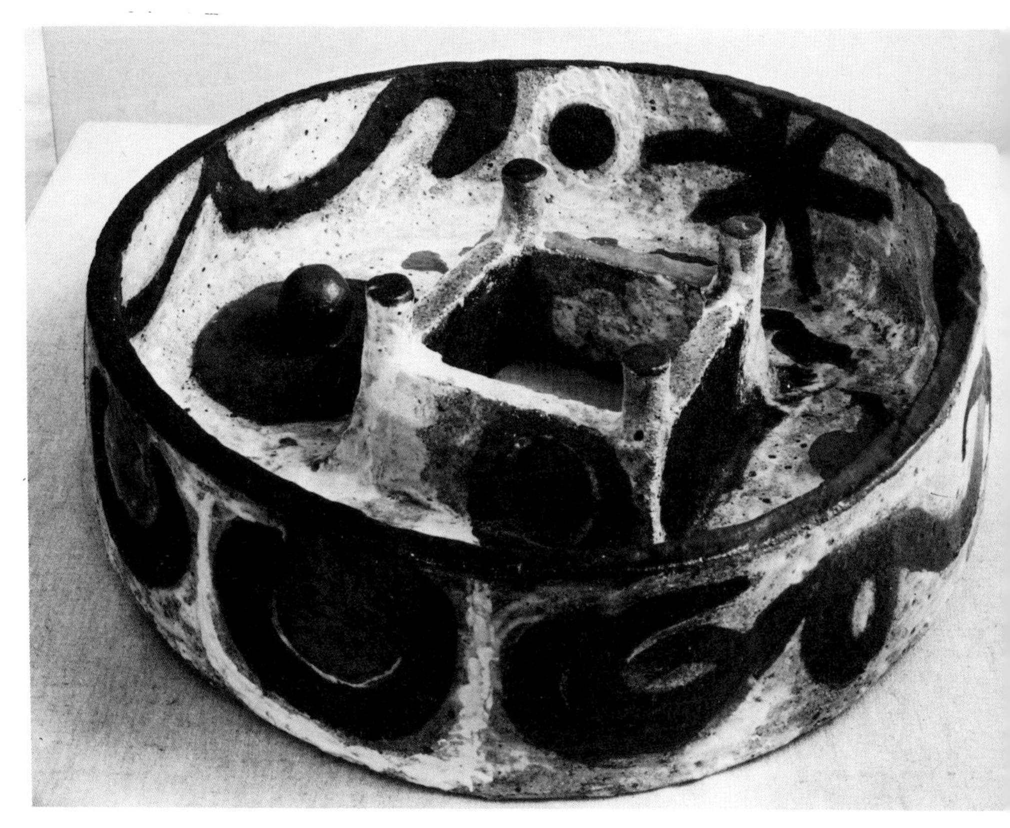

Miró and Artigas
Architecture
1962

and mysterious points punctuating the walls of Lascaux. Miró's studio was also a cave where he recreated for himself the shadowy void of prehistory in order to detach himself from the chain of "art history." If he was thinking of something as he painted, it was prehistory. Yet he never imitated its figures; and, in *Bullfight*, his bull does not resemble those at Lascaux any more than it does Picasso's.

In 1968, Miró's signs began struggling, contorting, and hitting each other as if they were waging war in the cosmogonic field of the picture. In *Figures and Birds Celebrating the Coming Night*, *Flight of Birds Around the Woman with Three Hairs in the Moonlight*, *Woman and Birds*, and *Woman and Birds in the Night*, we are introduced to a struggle that continued in 1969, and after. In it, the spirit of Dada fused with the precise, anonymous gestures of the painters of prehistory. This fusion was not a reconciliation, but rather the result of an enormous expenditure of energy overflowing everywhere at once—anonymously. Up to the end, Miró sought everything *except* the easy way out. The unpredictable flight of birds in space, their entangled trajectories and sudden landings are the definitive "models" of his expression, which freed itself from the memory of its past and always refused the temptations of style and ornament. In 1973, working on badly damaged cardboard and devastated, violently burned canvas, Miró deconstructed his vocabulary in the dream of a total destruction of all codes of communication. From 1968 to his death in 1982, his humans and animals completely left the realm of figuration; the savage, erring lines that evoke them destroy the very idea of representation. Miró showed only his own violent energy, directed against all forms of order, including the order that personal stylistic harmony creates. He listened to Karlheinz Stockhausen's music, and recognized something of himself in it; but his own storms and devastation were never enough. It seemed as if the only thing left animating him was a silent, electric rage against his own position as a great, internationally famous painter. Furiously, like Picasso, he completely deconstructed the image of his work, refusing in advance to let posterity tame him.

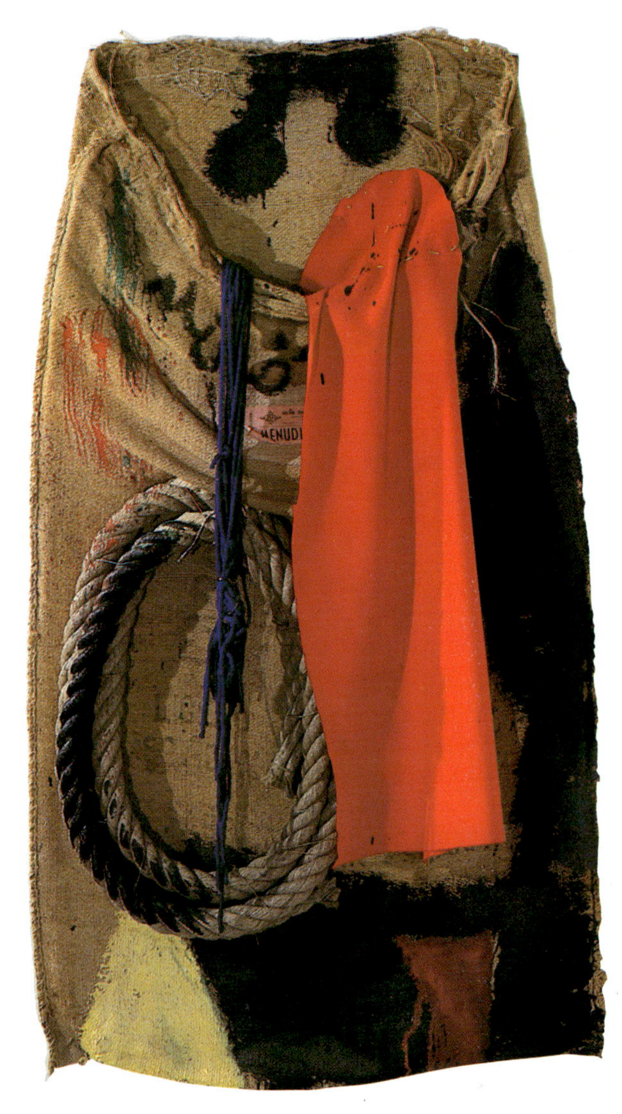

Sobreteixim
1973

Miró could never accept the art market or the fact that his works were transformed into financial capital and confiscated by banker-collectors: "Now, what disgusts me the most," he told Georges Raillard, "are the guys who buy paintings as investments. It just disgusts me. And it happens all the time! ... In any case, I would rather see my paintings in museums than in some financier's dining room or living room." Miró did not deconstruct his vocabulary because of the astronomical sums his works fetched; but his obsession with destruction did coincide with the commercial success of his work, especially after 1968. It would be a travesty of truth not to say so. This explains why such an admired and beloved painter felt such joy in dilapidation and violence, as if he were taking his revenge for the original reasons of his success, linked to the image of the innocent, naive, childish, and harmless painter he could not shake: "Yes, my reputation bothers me enormously," he said. "We were talking about intellectual laziness. That's what it is. People don't have the strength to understand others." Nothing could be more unlike the "innocent" games of childhood than the paintings, engravings, and sculptures he realized during the last fifteen years of his life. He stopped at nothing to make his scream of refusal and disgust heard and keep from being confused with the troop of painters who are all too happy to let their work be transformed into merchandise. Some day we will have to analyze the content and form of our century's greatest works in function of the various attitudes their makers adopted toward the art market. Along with Picasso, Miró, who defined himself as a man in revolt against "the world as we know it," would, without a doubt, shed the most light on this issue.

If, as he wrote in the *Catalan Notebooks* in 1940-1941, Miró once wanted to paint the "beginnings of a form of expression that will later emerge from the catastrophe and ruins of the present age," if he wanted his "works to be conceived with a fiery soul, but realized with clinical coldness," it was because, during the war, he still hoped that the world was going to change and, eventually, be radically transformed. But, like several other Surrealists, he had to admit that, in spite of the apparent success of their ideas, the economic system behind the old values was only strengthened and toughened as things returned to "normal" after the war. As successful as he was powerless, what choice did he have but to revolt against the matter and language of his own works and explode their silent enigma by tearing them apart? But when he did, he brought a new glory to matter itself, quite independent of the notions of art and artwork. As he himself wrote: "My figurations arose out of matter, just as Hölderlin's thought arose out of *speech*."

The voice of matter, created out of a permanent contact and unremitting confrontation with it, Miró's works are anything *but* idealistic. They began in automatism "to stimulate thought," which then, in turn, acted in the realm of matter. They are not a mirror moving along the road and flattering reality and history, nor are they a mere advertisement for self or proclamation of personal power. Dynamized by a need to supply the mental means to resist all slogans and tyrannies, Miró's works make a statement and create an adventure. They are a map drawn to orient their viewers in the fighting dance that makes a man or woman something other than a cog: the map of a cosmogony and its catastrophes, meant to make us realize that we must not submit. Miró is not just a radically new way of looking, but a revolution in painting, a Surrealist revolution in the folds of Surrealism: a die that has escaped from the cup and will never go back, a shooting star in search of another constellation, mapping the unmappable, the comets that traverse us all.

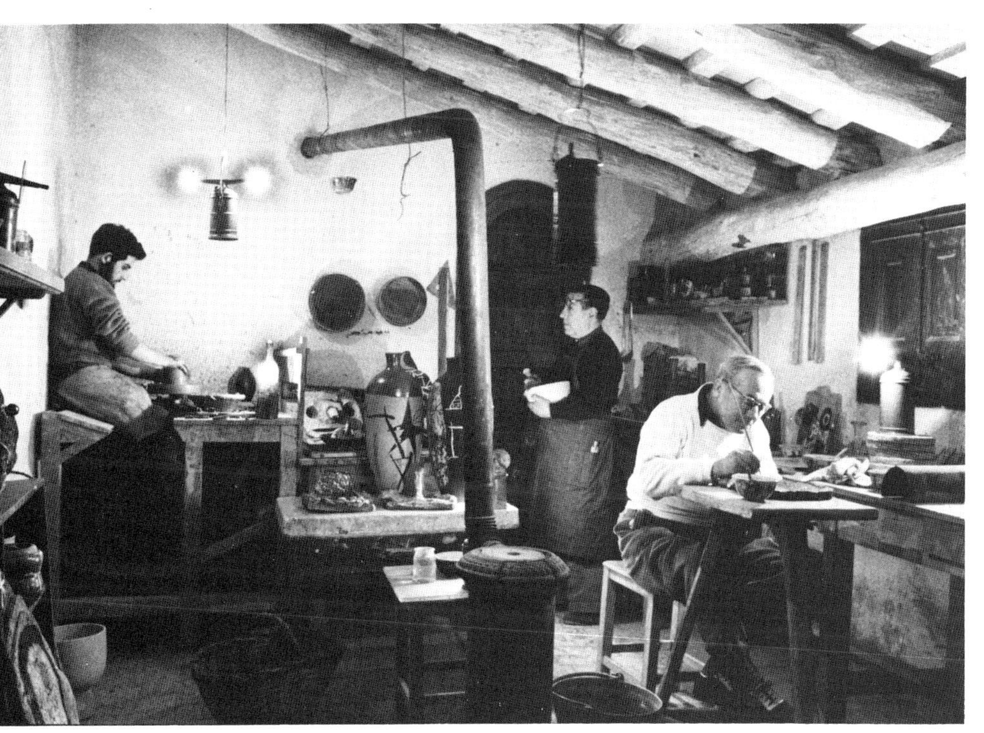

Joan Gardy Artigas,
Josef L. Artigas,
Joan Miró
1956

1893
Birth of Joan Miró in Barcelona on April 20, at 4 Pasaje del Credito, near the Plaza Reale.
His father, a goldsmith and watchmaker, was a native of the Tarragona region; his mother was the daughter of a cabinetmaker in Palma de Mallorca.
"Many aspects of Miró's character belong to the psychology of the Catalans or cannot be explained without it. Miró himself was always proud of his Catalan origins and refused to be considered only as a Spanish painter" (J. Dupin).
Miró spent his childhood and teenage years in Barcelona and at his grandparents' houses. Although he spent a good many years in Paris (1920-1940), Miró's real turf was always Montroig, Barcelona, and Palma. "We Catalans think you have to have your feet solidly planted on the ground before you can leap into the air" (statement to J. J. Sweeney).
1900
Enters the Calle Regomir school and takes optional drawing classes.
1905
First sketchbooks. Mostly drawings of the Catalan countryside.
1907
His father forces him to enter a business college; but he also attends the Lonja School of Fine Arts, where Picasso had studied ten years earlier.
1910
Miró abandons his art studies and gets a job as a clerk in a trading company. During this gloomy period, he falls seriously ill and goes to Montroig to recuperate. His convalescence will be a rebirth.
1912
Having overcome his father's resistance, he enrolls in Francisco Gali's Escola d'Art. Gali closely follows the progress of his new student, whose classmates think him hopelessly awkward, but in whom Gali senses something exceptional.
1915
He starts going to an independent drawing academy, the Sant Lluch circle, set up on the premises of the "4 Gats" cabaret that Picasso made famous. First studio. He shares in the new excitement of the Barcelona art scene, the center of which is the Dalmau Gallery.
1916
He shows several of his works to Dalmau, who offers encouragement. Fauve landscapes. Highly aware of the new trends in art, Miró assimilates them slowly as he continues his own investigations.
1917
First exhibition at the Dalmau Gallery. Meets Picabia.
1918
In the summer, he begins working on meticulous landscapes that will lead him out of Fauvism to *The Farm* (1920-1921), which sums up his early investigations and indicates what will follow. Like Artigas, a member of the "agrupaccio

Courbet," which includes the most advanced young Catalan painters.

1919

First trip to Paris, where he meets Picasso. "Paris has completely overwhelmed me—and in a beneficial way. Like living flesh, I feel that I have been penetrated by this city's gentle kiss," he wrote to his friend Rafols.

1920

Moves to Paris and encounters hardship and difficulties. Near the end of the year, he finds a studio on the Rue Blomet, next door to André Masson. The Rue Blomet quickly becomes the home of a happy community of artists, visited by Leiris, Desnos, Artaud, and Limbour. Miró also meets Max Jacob, Pierre Reverdy, and Tristan Tzara.

1921

Exhibition at the Galerie de la Licorne, with a preface by Maurice Raynal. Unsuccessful.

1922

Ernest Hemingway buys *The Farm*. End of the "realist" period.

1923-1924

The period of what Jacques Dupin calls the "revelation." Miró crosses the threshold, and becomes Miró, in *The Tilled Field*, painted during the summer in Montroig: a release of the enormous energy that had built up in the artist in the highly charged Parisian atmosphere.

1924

Miró's "tumultuous entry" (André Breton) into the Surrealist group, where he will be more a fellow traveler than devoted disciple. From this time on, in spite of perpetual crises and doubts, Miró's work will develop as an enormous "work in progress" based on unchanging themes.

1925

Exhibition at the Galerie Pierre, with a text written by Benjamin Péret. Scandal and success. Miró has "made it," but the paintings he is then doing are perhaps his most secret and silent.

1926

Works with Max Ernst on the sets for the Ballets Russes' *Romeo and Juliet*.

1927

Moves to Montmartre.

1928

Trip to Holland. Series of "Dutch Interiors." Major exhibition at the Galerie Bernheim. André Breton publishes *Le Surréalisme et la peinture*.

1929

Marries Pilar Juncosa in Palma. Series of "Imaginary Portraits."

1930

Another exhibition at the Galerie Pierre. First exhibition in the United States. Lithographs for Tzara's *L'Arbre des voyageurs*.

1931

Birth of his daughter Dolorès. Sculpture-objects.

1932

Exhibitions at the Galerie Pierre in Paris and the Pierre Matisse Gallery in New York.

1933
First etchings. Drawing-collages. Large paintings based on collages.
1934
Paintings on sandpaper. Beginning of the "wild period."
1935
Participates in the Surrealist exhibition organized in Tenerife (Canary Islands).
1936-1940
Miró stops going to Spain.
1937
Designs the poster "Aidez l'Espagne" and does a mural painting for the pavilion of the Spanish Republic at the Paris World's Fair. A brief and violent foray into "tragic realism."
1938
Returns to a more serene kind of painting. Spends his first summer at Varengeville-sur-Mer.
1940
Begins the "Constellations," his exemplary work, at Varengeville. Returns to Spain after the German invasion of France.
1941
Finishes the "Constellations." A major retrospective of his work is held at the Museum of Modern Art in New York. J. J. Sweeney publishes the first monograph on Miró.
1944
Death of the artist's mother. First ceramics with Artigas. "I was seduced by the dazzle of ceramic: it's like sparks of fire," he told Yvan Taillandier. Ceramics and sculpture will play an important role in the development of his work after the war, not to mention a profusion of lithographs.
1947
First trip to the United States. First exhibition at the Galerie Maeght. From this time on, Miró will be exhibited throughout the world; and publications concerning his work will soon become too numerous to keep track of.
1950
Moves from the Pasaje del Credito, where he had returned during the war, to the Calle Folgarolas.
1954
First prize in engraving at the Venice Biennale.
1954-1956
Ceramic projects with Artigas.
1956
Leaves Barcelona for Palma, where his architect friend Jose Luis Sert designs his new studio.
1958
Ceramic walls for UNESCO headquarters in Paris.
1959
Second trip to the United States.
1961
Publication of Jacques Dupin's major monograph.
1964
Opening of the Fondation Maeght in Saint-Paul-de-Vence, the tone of which is powerfully set by Miró's "labyrinth."

1966
Travels to Japan for a major retrospective of his work.
1970
Ceramic mural for the airport in Barcelona.
1972-1973
Exhibition of the "Sobreteixims" in Barcelona and Paris.
1975
Opening of the Miró Foundation, a center for contemporary art designed by J. L. Sert, in Barcelona.
During Franco's last years in power, Miró actively supports the regime's opponents.
1978
Monumental sculpture for La Défense, near Paris. Major retrospective in Madrid.
1983
Miró dies on Christmas Day.

BIBLIOGRAPHY

Since James Johnson Sweeney's pioneering effort in 1941 (reprinted, New York, 1969), a great variety of monographs have been devoted to Miró. Of these, the most important is Jacques Dupin's *Joan Miró* (Paris, 1961; New York, 1962), an expanded edition of which is scheduled for publication. Also noteworthy are Pere Gimferrer's *Miró, catalan universel* (Barcelona, 1978), Alain Jouffroy and Joan Teixidor's *Miró sculptures* (Paris, 1974), José Pierre and Jose Corredor-Matheos's *Miró-Artigas, céramiques* (Paris, 1974), and *Miró et Mallorca* (Paris, 1985), all of which are still in print.

Miró's statements and writings have been published by Yvon Taillandier (*Je travaille comme un jardinier*, Paris, 1964), Gaëtan Picon (*Carnets catalans*, Geneva, 1976), and Georges Raillard (*Ceci est la couleur de mes rêves*, Paris, 1977).

Of the many prefaces, articles, and poetic texts on Miró's work, we will mention the "historic" texts written by André Breton (in *Le Surréalisme et la peinture*, new edition, Paris, 1966) and Michel Leiris (republished in *Brises*, Paris, 1966; and in Joan Miró, New York, 1972); but it should be remembered that Benjamin Péret, René Char, Jacques Prévert, Paul Eluard, and Tristan Tzara also wrote important pieces on Miró. Since World War II, texts by Dupin,

Jouffroy, Yves Bonnefoy, Dore Ashton, Walter Erben, Clement Greenberg, Roland Penrose, and David Sylvester deserve attention.
The only *catalogue raisonné* concerns the lithographs.

Finally, Miró illustrated a number of literary works. These much-sought-after books include:
Tristan Tzara, *L'Arbre des voyageurs*, éd. de la Montagne, Paris, 1930.
Georges Hugnet, *Enfances*, Cahiers d'Art, Paris, 1933.
Benjamin Péret, *Au paradis des fantômes*, Henri Parisot, Paris, 1938.
Série de Barcelone, Joan Prats, Barcelona, 1944.
Tristan Tzara, *L'Antitête*, Bordas, Paris, 1948.
Album 13, Maeght, Paris, 1948.
Tristan Tzara, *Parler seul*, Maeght, Paris, 1950.
René Crevel, *La Bague d'aurore*, Louis Broder, Paris, 1958.
Paul Eluard, *A toute épreuve*, Gérald Cramer, Geneva, 1958.
René Char, *Nous avons*, Louis Broder, Paris, 1959.
Je travaille comme un jardinier, interviews by Yvon Taillandier, XXe siècle, Paris, 1963.
Alfred Jarry, *Ubu roi*, Teriade, Paris, 1964.
Quelques fleurs pour des amis, with a text by Eugène Ionesco, XXe siècle, Paris, 1965.
Hommage à Joan Prats, Poligrafa, Barcelona, 1971.
Joan Miró, *Le Lézard aux plumes d'or*, a poem written and illustrated by the artist, Louis Broder, Paris, 1971.
Alain Jouffroy, *Liberté des libertés*, Soleil Noir, Paris, 1971.

ILLUSTRATIONS

69 : *Figures in Nature*, 1935, oil on canvas, 75×100 cm., Arensberg Collection, Philadelphia Museum of Art, Philadelphia.

70 : *Self Portrait*, 1937-1960, oil and pencil on canvas, 146×97 cm., Joan Miró Foundation, Barcelona.

72 : *Seated Woman I*, 1938, oil on canvas, 162×130 cm., The Museum of Modern Art, New York.

73 : *Seated Woman II*, 1939, oil on canvas, 162×130 cm., Peggy Guggenheim Foundation, Venice.

76 : *Three Figures on a Black Ground*, 1934, gouache on paper, 50×60 cm., Musée d'Art moderne, Villeneuve-d'Ascq.

78 : *The Beautiful Bird Revealing the Unknown to a Couple in Love* (from the "Constellations" series), 1941, gouache and oil wash on paper, 45.9×58.1 cm., The Museum of Modern Art, New York.

79 : *Women Encircled by the Flight of a Bird* (from the "Constellations" series), 1940, gouache and oil wash on paper, 45.5×35.5 cm., Elisa Breton Collection, Paris.

81 : *The Smile with Blazing Wings*, 1953, oil on canvas, 33×46 cm., private collection, Palma de Mallorca.

86 : *The Wind-Clock*, 1967, bronze, 49×30×16 cm., Galerie Maeght-Lelong, Paris. Photo: Claude Gaspari.

87 : *Woman and Bird*, 1968, bronze, 32.5×25.5×15 cm., Galerie Maeght-Lelong, Paris. Photo: Claude Gaspari.

89 : Porcelain, 1981, 17.5×7×6 cm., Galerie Maeght-Lelong, Paris.

90 : *Bird Nesting in Fingers in Bloom*, 1969, bronze, 81×46×25 cm., Parellada Foundry, Barcelona. Photo: F. Catala Roca.

92-93 : *Man and Woman in the Night*, 1969, painted bronze, 78×45×45 cm., 87×32×32 cm., Maeght Foundation, Saint-Paul-de-Vence. Photo: Claude Gaspari.

95 : *Object of Sunset*, 1937, sculpture-object, painted trunk und metal elements, 68×44×26 cm., Musée national d'Art moderne, Paris.

97 : *Woman with Dishevelled Hair*, 1968, marble, Maeght Foundation, Saint-Paul-de-Vence.

100 : *Pitchfork*, 1963, iron and bronze, 507×455×9 cm., Maeght Foundation, Saint-Paul-de-Vence.

102 : *Birds of Prey Swooping down on Our Shadows*, 1970, oil on cowhide, 250×200 cm., Galerie Maeght-Lelong, Paris.

105 : *Blue II*, 1961, oil on canvas, 270×355 cm., Musée national d'Art moderne, Paris.

106 : Miró and Artigas, *Architecture*, 1962, ceramics, 15×63 cm.

108 : *Sobreteixim*, 1973, 140×80 cm., Galerie Maeght-Lelong, Paris.

111 : Joan Gardy Artigas, Josef L. Artigas, Joan Miró, 1956. Photo: Sabine Weiss, Rapho.

Cover: *Hand Catching a Bird*, 1926, oil on canvas. Photo: Jacqueline Hyde.